CW00418215

The Pilgrim's Psalmgress

A devotional look at selected psalms through the eyes
of the Pilgrim's Progress

by

Gary Stevens

Cover picture: Hamford backwater by Hannah Stevens

Thanks to...

This little book has been many years in the writing and owes its existence, and therefore my thanks, to many people. First of all to my Aunties Reta and Jean who gave me my first copy of Pilgrim's Progress as a boy. Then to my lecturer in English, Dr. Caroline Phillips, who taught me how to read and understand poetry. Then to Pastor Brian Thompson who taught me the imperative of preaching Jesus from the psalms.

Then, thanks to Peter Cordle who, after many discouragements in the producing of the book, encouraged me to believe that this book had a message that others would want to read. Finally, thanks to David Lowbridge who actually took the text and made it into what you hold in your hands.

I offer my heartfelt thanks and gratitude to you all, and dedicate this book to all who have loved me and encouraged me on my pilgrimage, but most of all to the Lord of the Journey.

Introduction

The story of Pilgrim's Progress is, after the Holy Bible, the most widely read book in the world. It has been translated into many languages and there is a veritable body of work of commentaries, interpretations and opinions that issue forth upon it. The outline of the story is on the next pages for those who have never read it or want a quick reminder.

My purpose in writing this little book is to make the story of the pilgrim known to a new audience, and to show how relevant it is to all of us. No book becomes the world's second best seller unless it has a resonance with men and women of all types and ages. Its message is as relevant now as it was when it was written, and perhaps more so as we see society in general and haters of Christianity in particular, close the net of our freedoms which we have enjoyed for so many years in order to do everything they can to rid our country and culture of everything the Bible stands for, and punish and persecute Christians who will continue to proclaim its truth.

That leads us to the story's basic theme: The Christian is a pilgrim in an alien and hostile world. That is the clear teaching of the Bible. "This world is not our home, we are just passing through," says the old song. We are on a pilgrimage "from this world to that which is to come", and we have the bible as our map and the Lord as our guide. We may be few; we may be constantly going contrary to the majority, but we go on nonetheless. We are to go on in a spirit of excitement as our destination gets ever closer: we are to even rejoice in our trials. We are never to be ashamed to tell all about why we are going and where we are going. In fact we are to act as Evangelist did and point the way out to all who will listen.

· And as we go, our relationship with Jesus should be just that: a daily experience and interaction with the Son of God who loved us and gave himself for us. He has promised to never leave or forsake us: he will be with us wherever we go.

All scripture was written to teach, to correct and to train in righteousness everyone who will submit to its message, and the Psalms are a part of that scripture. The difference with the Psalms is that they are songs and poems and proverbs all in one book and their fundamental purpose is to help us worship the Lord. Gareth Crossley writes: *The 150 psalms make a unique contribution to the Scriptures. Here are instructions as to how God is to be worshipped and adored....; here are profound insights into the person and work of the Saviour; and here the deepest spiritual experiences of the human heart.*[1]

---

[1] p464

What I have sought to do is to pick out the major adventures / themes of the Pilgrim's journey and link them to our experiences as pilgrims using a psalm that teaches us about that theme. It is awe-inspiring to think upon the fact that our pilgrimage is a unique journey that will be written, not by Bunyan, but in God's book; a journey that will be our experiences of God and the conflict and deliverance which he promises.

My prayer as I send this book out into the reading world is two-fold: Firstly I hope that the reader who is not yet a Christian will find Christ in these pages and begin that journey. Secondly I hope that the reader who is my fellow pilgrim will be refreshed as you go on your journey to the Celestial City.

The Story of Pilgrim's Progress

The writer tells us that he fell asleep in the wilderness and dreamed of a man named Christian, who was tormented by spiritual anguish. A spiritual guide named Evangelist visits Christian and urges him to leave the City of Destruction. Evangelist tells him that salvation can only be found in the Celestial City.

Christian begs his family to accompany him, but they scorn the idea, and he leaves alone. On his way, Christian falls into a bog called the Slough of Despond, but he is saved. He meets Worldly Wiseman, who tells him he can lead a happy existence without religion. Refusing, Christian is sheltered in Goodwill's house. Goodwill tells Christian to stop by the Interpreter's home, where Christian learns many lessons about the journey.

Walking along the wall of Salvation, Christian sees Christ's tomb and cross. At this place his burden falls to the ground. One of the three Shining Ones, celestial creatures, hands him a rolled certificate for entry to the Celestial City. Christian falls asleep and loses his certificate. After great self reproach and by retracing his tracks, he eventually finds the certificate. Walking on, Christian meets the four mistresses of the Palace Beautiful, who provide him shelter.

They also feed him and arm him. After descending the Valley of Humiliation, Christian meets the monster Apollyon, who tries to kill him. Christian is armed, and he strikes Apollyon with a sword and then proceeds through the desert-like Valley of the Shadow of Death toward the Celestial City.

Christian meets Faithful, a pilgrim from his hometown. Faithful and Christian are joined by a third pilgrim, Talkative, whom Christian spurns. Evangelist arrives and warns Faithful and Christian about the wicked town of Vanity, which they will soon enter. Evangelist foretells that either Christian or Faithful will die in Vanity.

The two enter Vanity and visit its famous fair. They resist temptation and are mocked by the townspeople. Eventually the citizens of Vanity imprison Christian and Faithful for mocking their local religion. Faithful defends himself at his trial and is executed, rising to heaven after death. Christian is remanded to prison but later escapes and continues his journey.

Another fellow pilgrim named Hopeful befriends Christian on his way. On their journey, a pilgrim who uses religion as a means to get ahead in the world, named By-ends, crosses their path. Christian rejects his company. The two enter the plain of Ease, where a smooth talker named Demas tempts them with silver. Christian and Hopeful pass him by.

Leaving the path they should be on the pilgrims end up taking shelter for the night on the grounds of Doubting Castle. Because they have trespassed they are captured by the castle's owner, the Giant Despair, who, with the encouragement of his wife, imprisons and tortures them. Christian and Hopeful escape when they remember they possess the key of Promise, which unlocks any door in Despair's domain.

Proceeding onward, Christian and Hopeful approach the Delectable Mountains near the Celestial City. They encounter wise shepherds who warn them of the treacherous mountains Error and Caution, where previous pilgrims have died. The shepherds point out pilgrims who wander among tombs nearby, having been blinded by the Giant Despair. They warn the pilgrims to beware of shortcuts, which may be paths to hell.

The two pilgrims meet Ignorance, a sprightly lad who believes that living a good life is sufficient to prove one's religious faith. Christian refutes him, and Ignorance decides to avoid their company. The pilgrims also meet Flatterer, who snares them in a net, and Atheist, who denies that the Celestial City exists. Crossing the sleep-inducing Enchanted Ground, they try to stay awake by discussing Hopeful's sinful past and religious doctrine.

Christian and Hopeful gleefully approach the land of Beulah, where the Celestial City is located. The landscape teems with flowers and fruit, and the pilgrims are refreshed. To reach the gate into the city, they must first cross a river without a bridge. Christian, thinking he is unworthy at the end to receive his Lord's favour, nearly drowns in despair, but Hopeful reminds him of Christ's love, and Christian emerges safely from the water. The residents of the Celestial City joyously welcome the two pilgrims.

Contents Page

Chapter 1

Let the journey begin

Please read Psalm 1

John Bunyan wrote a story about a man called Graceless. This man realised one day that something was wrong with his life. He had a family, a home, friends and many others things besides, yet he lacked a peace inside. There was a longing that these things could not satisfy. He knew somehow that all was not well with his soul: that he was condemned, as was the whole city in which he lived and all the people amongst whom he lived. He had to flee, but he didn't know why, or where to go, or who to go to. No one could help him: when he told them of this burden, even his own kith and kin dismissed it, then laughed at him, got irritated with him and finally despised him. But Graceless then met a man who pointed out to him that he had to flee from the wrath to come and begin a journey – a journey that would cure his soul. And so he went out, although not knowing really where he was going and definitely not knowing what would happen on the way.

Reader, I ask you a question you may have asked yourself: perhaps it is partly why you have picked up this book. *Is all well with your soul?* This of course leads on to other questions: Do you know you have a soul? You may also ask: What is the soul? It is that invisible part of you that is in essence - *you*. It is the bit that thinks, that feels, that knows, that hopes – all that which is indefinable and yet all that which is uniquely you. More than this, it is the part of you that is eternal, for it is the very breath of God in you. Your soul needs and longs for God, but cannot find Him, because it has been cut off by your rejection of God and his demands upon your life. On one hand, part of you wants independence from God, and the freedom to control your own life – yet on the other hand, inside you there is a part that longs for reconciliation with God – for your spirit and his to be united again. And that is why the journey begins. It is something you cannot manufacture and you cannot ignore. Start the journey with this psalm.

What is this psalm about? This psalm talks about two groups of people in the world. There are only these two groups as far as this psalm is concerned, as far as the bible is concerned, and as far therefore, as God is concerned. To sum it up in the words of a preacher of long ago, it is about: "Two men, two ways, two ends." What are these two groups – how are they classified – what makes me belong to one or the other and how do I know which one I belong to, are all questions you might be asking? This psalm answers all these questions, and so when you have read it, ask yourself honestly, which group am I in? Why: because if you are in one group you have started the journey, and if you are in the other you *desperately* need to start the journey just as Graceless did – for you too are Graceless in the story.

Blessed

Let me start with a note of introduction. This psalm is the first of the 150 psalms. It may or may not be the first one written, but the editor of the book decided to put it first to introduce the theme of the Psalms: there are righteous people and there are unrighteous people in the world. At the start of the psalms, as at the start of your journey to Heaven, you must face this question; which am I? Every man is either right with God (i.e. righteous), or they are not (i.e. unrighteous). How can we know what a righteous man is like? Firstly he is *blessed.* The word here simply means happy, and has as its root a word that means straight, level or right. Imagine a building that is made completely true to its blueprint. Its corners are right angles; its sides are straight, its roof is squarely placed on the walls. The whole thing fits together and is right. It is strong; it is able to withstand the rigors of the harshest weather. It looks right, and it is right because it is built right. Its builder can sit back and admire his handiwork, as he sees that it is foursquare. God looks at us – his creatures – and he can look at some people, and pronounce them spiritually foursquare – righteous. God takes great delight in these people; he loves them, cherishes them and has a day-to-day relationship with them. He knows them, and they have the inestimable privilege of knowing him. Notice that this state of affairs is a constant one: *Blessed is the man* - not "was" or "will be", but a constant is. He is always blessed, always in this state: nothing can separate him from it.

But not everybody is blessed. *The ungodly are not so* (v4). C. H. Spurgeon notes that the Septuagint Old Testament (Greek Version) translates it more forcibly: *Not so, the ungodly, not so.*[2] There is this double negative used here. He is an unhappy man spiritually. He may experience pleasures in his life, and enjoy many things but the psalmist is not talking about emotion. He is talking about his status in life. He in God's eyes, to use the building analogy, is twisted, out of shape. He is not fit for the purpose for which he was made; instead he has become deformed and ugly. Thus the builder has no choice but to knock it down. The unrighteous man is God's enemy, and God is his enemy.

So, Psalm 1 teaches that you are either righteous or unrighteous in your standing or, to put it another way, your

---

[2] Treasury of David, Volume I, p3

position before God. God is either delighted in you or angry with you. What is for sure is that God is not indifferent about you. You are not lost in the crowd. That is both comforting and frightening. It is comforting because if you are in God's household you are of all people most blessed: you have God as your father and your friend. But if you are ungodly in God's eyes you are in a terrible, terrible situation: God is your enemy and he is the deadliest foe - ever.

Listening and doing

So, you are either righteous or unrighteous. But how can you know what you are? Notice how astute the psalm is. The key to identifying what anybody is like is to look at what he or she enjoys. The righteous man **listens** to God. He obeys God. He is content with what God has made him, and where God has put him. *His delight is in the law of the Lord, and in his law he meditates day and night.* The righteous man understands that he needs the word of God for his soul, just as he needs food and drink for his body. Jesus Christ said: *man shall not live by bread alone but by every word that proceeds from the mouth of God*[3] – in other words; the bible. The righteous man wants to know what God wants him to know. He is interested in God's words, God's ideas and God's priorities. He wants to know what God is like. He is

---

[3] Matthew chapter 4 v 4

interested in what God is doing; what God has done and what God will do in the future. All these things and more are found in God's word. If he doesn't read it he'll never know. But he doesn't just casually read God's word; he meditates on it. He reads it regularly, carefully and thoughtfully. He asks it questions, and studies for the answers; he commits it to memory – it becomes his daily companion. If you are a righteous person you will read God's word like this, so ask yourself: Do you read God's word like this?

Why does the righteous man read the bible so often and so earnestly? Why is he so dependent on it? It is because he wants to do what God tells him he should do, and shun what God tells him to shun. This is said in a negative form; by what the righteous man does not do. He (unlike the unrighteous man) *does not walk in the counsel of the ungodly.*

There are many counsellors in this life aren't there? Plenty of people who try to influence what you say, or think, or wear, or go to. Others will tell you who to admire, or copy. We have "role models" in our society. These are people whom we are supposed to look up to and try to be like. Sadly many role models are no example at all. All too often they display their selfishness, immorality, rebelliousness and folly for all to see, and come to a sticky end. The righteous man will not listen to people like this. He does not walk in the counsel of the ungodly. But here the unrighteous man goes wrong. He listens to wrong advice, he fills his mind with wrong ideas, he doesn't bother to check to see what God is saying, and so he ends up defaulting on God and counting his word as of no value.

The righteous man does not: *stand in the path of sinners.* In other words the righteous man will not go where the sinner goes. This does not mean he goes off and retires to a cave. It means he is not found enjoying sinful practices with like-minded ungodly men. The righteous man can and will enjoy many lawful pleasures in this world, but he will not be found drifting into indulging in the sinful habits and wicked practices of the ungodly. The reason for this is a powerful one. Having read what pleases God, the righteous man shuns the wrong and chooses the right. I emphasise this: the righteous man is not a naïveté: he is one who fully understands the choice he has. He deliberately shuns the evil and chooses the good: he has the inner strength to do so. Can you say that about your conduct?

Nor sits in the seat of the scornful. He who started off walking with, listening to, the ungodly, soon regresses to being where they are, doing what they do. He ends up at ease with them – in fact becomes one of them – who mock God, his words, ways and people. He is doing all that the wicked do for he is one of them. *Be not deceived,* wrote the apostle Paul, *bad company corrupts good habits*[4]. The Lord Jesus said: *It is by their fruits you shall know them.*[5]

Producing

Having seen that whom a man heeds and what a man does defines him, we now turn to the third mark of a man. It is what God thinks of him that ultimately decides whether a man is godly or ungodly. A righteous man is at peace with how God has made him, and where God has put him. He has a reason for living; he has a purpose. Here is an illustration of what that is like: *He shall be like a tree, planted by the rivers of water; that brings forth his fruit in due season, whose leaf shall not wither, and whatever he does shall prosper* (v3). This picture of the tree is perceptive.

The tree is planted	- It is where God has put him
It brings forth fruit	- It serves its purpose
The tree is... by the waterside	- It is provided and cared for
It's leaf shall not wither	- It prospers

All these things flow from God's dealing with the righteous man. God blesses him. God prospers him. He knows his walk; he takes care of him on the journey to Heaven.

But the unrighteous man is not planted anywhere for he has no roots in God. He thus reaps what he sows. It is the

---

[4] I Corinthians 15 v 33
[5] Matthew 7 v 20

fool who says and lives as if there is no God. He is not welcomed into Heaven. How can he spend eternity with the God he has steadfastly ignored while on earth? There is no spiritual fruit on their ear of corn. They are all husk; all chaff. When the winds of death and judgement blow they are forever cast on the breeze. As the righteous go into eternal life, so the unrighteous go forever with no blessing, no home and no comfort to everlasting destruction. Because your soul is eternal – like God who made it – it can never cease to be. Therefore you will either be in eternal paradise with God or eternal condemnation – banished from the presence of God.

This psalm teaches us that your attitude to the bible is crucial to your standing with God and to what God thinks of you. Your attitude to the bible determines what counsel you listen to – the ungodly or God. Your attitude to the bible determines what rule you live your life by – a wrong code of conduct or God's Ten Commandments. Your attitude to the Word of God determines what God thinks of you. The New Testament teaches us plainly that the Lord Jesus Christ is the Word of God[6]. He is God's last word to mankind[7]. Ultimately to reject the bible is to reject Christ. To reject Christ is to reject the way to Heaven that God offers, and

[6] John 1 vv 1-3, 14
[7] Hebrews 1 vv 1-3

the only way that a man can be righteous at all. Psalm 1 asks you are you righteous or unrighteous – godly or ungodly?

So have you started the journey? Is God's word your guide to life? If not you must, like Graceless in the story, flee from the wrath to come, for you stand condemned where you are, and you must do something to save your soul. If you were in a house that was on fire you would do whatever it took to escape and live wouldn't you? How much more your eternal soul, which now stands in danger of hell fire? Flee from the wrath to come while there is still time. In this chapter we have seen **why** we must start the journey. The next question is **where** we must start. We start by fleeing from the wrath of God and fleeing into the arms of God.

Blessed is he who does not walk
With ungodly men, or heed their talk.
Nor stand under the sinner's nose
Nor mock with them that God oppose.

The godly man has one delight:
To read God's word both day and night.
By rivers of water, planted he,
Is made by God a fruitful tree.

On judgement day, discerning wind
Will blow away the chaff who sinned.
The righteous, though, his way is known.
And so by God is welcomed home.

Chapter 2

The right road

Please read Psalm 19

In Bunyan's story the pilgrim flees from the City of his birth. Despite all efforts of his family to make him stay and give up this notion of going on a journey – he puts his fingers in his ears and runs away. At first he doesn't make a successful start, but after an adventure or two is directed to a place known as the house of the Interpreter. He is told that when he calls there he would be shown excellent things: things that would help him and prepare him for his journey.[8] Why does he need an Interpreter? An interpreter translates information from one language to another. This interpreter translates from one realm to another – from the human way of thinking to God's way of thinking. At the house of the Interpreter Graceless has to have his thinking changed. He needs to look again at what he sees and what he knows, and have it interpreted into the God given truth he has to receive. Up till now he has viewed things through the filter of his own mind and understanding and prejudices. Now he needs to think as God thinks and see as God sees. How is that going to happen? He has to start listening to God. If he

---

[8] The Pilgrim's Progress, p36

is to know God intimately – if he is to delight in God's law, he must begin to listen to what God has said and still says today. In this psalm we have God's message to man. But man needs to have ears that can hear God's message; eyes that can see God's message and a mind that can understand God message. But what is the message? It is here in Psalm 19. It is a truly wonderful psalm – so wonderful that he gave it to his chief musician to compose its melody.

God's message in creation

The first thing we read is that God made the world. Mankind has all sorts of speculative theories which last for a while and move on. But God's unchanging word tells us that God made all things, and that He reveals himself by what he has done. He is the wonderful Creator of an amazing universe: *the heavens declare the glory of God, and the firmament* [skies] *shows his handiwork.* To think that there is a person who created all things from nothing - **ex nihilo** - is just simply breathtaking. Notice too the way it is expressed. It is a commonly used idiom in the psalms where a statement is written and then added to or repeated by a second similar one. This method of writing reinforces the lesson. So we read: the heavens declare God's glory – his awesomeness, his supreme majesty. How? They do this because they are his handiwork. God made the skies, the stars and the planets.

Scientists tell us that there are millions upon millions upon millions of them – yet God knows them all by name. That is because he made them, shaped them and placed them. Notice the word *handiwork*. It is like someone sewing a small piece of embroidery, and displaying it. It shows their skill, their fine eye and talent. It is their handiwork – a small token of what they are really capable of. David is trying to find something to put God in perspective. Yet there is nothing as big as God: he both fills and transcends the universe; he never ends in time, or wisdom or power. The very heavens: all that there is in space above and around and beyond is but a piece of God's handiwork. This majestic God is the one who is speaking to you and to me.

Furthermore this message is unending. Day after day and night after night this message is being proclaimed, illustrating God's patience and faithfulness. All the time you are alive on earth you have God's message in front of you, telling you he is the majestic creator God. There is no one like him.

God's message is universal
There is no speech nor language where their voice is not heard. Their line is gone out through all the earth, and their words to the end of the world. The apostle Paul added many years later, *so that men are without excuse.*[9] Here is

an answer to a big question. Are all men accountable to God? What about those who have never read or heard God's message? David in this psalm and Paul in his letter to the Romans state very firmly that everyone has the voice and testimony of God in front of their eyes, there is no excuse not to know all about God and to worship him as God. Why then do we not see all men everywhere worshipping God? It has been often said that it is in man's nature to worship a god or gods. It is true but sadly not the true God. Mankind, Paul adds; *worship and serve the creature rather than the Creator.*[10] There are legions of religions, idols and gods; this has been so for thousands of years. In our own culture we elevate men to deity status – musicians, sports stars (think of the use of that word star!), writers, gurus, philosophers. They speak: we follow – we buy their books, their music or life-story, or else we change our homes or politics to imitate theirs. They are the topic of our conversation. They are in the newspapers and magazines. They fill our life. It is not that we do not worship. It is not even that we do not know we should worship God. It is that we have swapped the true God for gods of our own.

---

[9] Romans 1 v 20
[10] Romans 1 v 25

God's message is theological

God has not just told us of his existence; he has filled in many details. The heavens are not just a blank canvass. There is detail there. If you'll pardon the pun, we have a glorious visual aid in the sun. *Its rising is from one end of heaven and its circuit to the other end; and there is nothing hidden from its heat.* God has given us this visual aid to teach us more about himself. Consider the sun, the "strong man" of the skies, the star upon which our earth is utterly dependent. It rises, it warms the earth and it sets. Well what does it illustrate then?

It is a visual aid of God's <u>omnipresence</u>. The sun is not just shining in London; it is shining throughout England. It is not just shining in Paris, or Madrid; it is shining throughout Europe. Its light is everywhere this side of the planet. When it sets on this side it rises and does the same thing on the other. It is an illustration – but not a perfect one – that God is everywhere all at the same time. That is omnipresence.

The sun illustrates God's <u>providence</u>. God cares for his creation and provides for it. He uses the sun to keep life going on it. It warms the earth, it gives life and food to our planet; crops grow because of the sun, and when harvest time comes we can feed ourselves. It gives us light to see and helps keep us healthy. There are many ways in which the sun's light is vital to our well-being.

The utter reliability of the sun reminds us of God's faithfulness. The sun never fails to come back again! That would be unthinkable. God's faithfulness to our world is equally unfailing, more so in fact, because there will come a day when the sun won't shine and this world will pass away, but God will never cease to be.

The sun shows God's wisdom. How could life sustain itself on this earth without the sun? Yet the sun must be at the right circuit. If the sun was nearer, or further it would be no good to us: we would either burn or freeze. If its circuit were longer or shorter, day and night would be too long or too short and life cycles, so interdependent on earth would be in chaos.

I could go on, but stop for a moment, pause and wonder at the amazing way God has used the sun to teach mankind about Himself. Think about the fact that this psalm was written 3000 years ago, before modern science even worked out the earth was round or that the earth goes round the sun. What a great visual aid, what a teacher. What does the creation of God teach you? It shows enough for you to come to God and worship him, *the Creator who is blessed forever. Amen.*[11]

---

[11] Romans 1 v 25

God's message in his word

In this section of the psalm, David suddenly switches to a new way that God speaks: through his *law*. This word law stood for all the scriptures as they had been written at this time. Now we have a completed message from God – the bible. What is true of the first part of the work is true of the whole work. It is God's word – his letter, his story. If someone important writes to you, would you read it? How much more if the Supreme Creator pens a message – we had better read it very seriously and carefully. This cannot be understated in importance. We cannot ever hope to begin, let alone end our pilgrimage without the bible.

The purpose of this section is to tell us three things: that the scriptures are written by God; what the scriptures are in themselves, and what the effect will have upon the one who reads it. This section is made up of statements and each statement tells us these things in different ways:

God's message has status

Notice how David describes what the word of God actually is in and of itself: its status. What clout does it have? If someone were to ask you to describe the Bible's status you could list your answer like this:

- The word of God is *Law*, signifying its binding authority.

- The word of God is *Testimony*, signifying the legitimacy of its facts.

- The word of God is *Statute*, signifying its legal status.

- The word of God is *Command*, signifying its urgency.

- The word of God is *Fear*, signifying its weight and solemnity.

- The word of God is *Judgement,* signifying its timelessness and finality.

Each statement adds to and enriches the bald statement: *the bible is the word of God*. David describes it in many ways so that we have a clearer picture of just what we hold in our hands. It has ultimate status: a father's word has binding status in his own home; a council notice has binding status in its parish or borough; a judge's word has binding status in his own court. God's word has binding status throughout the universe.

God's message is wonderful

If I were to describe you, what would I say? What adjectives could I pick that might give a stranger some idea of what you are like as a person? What is God's word like? Is it harsh, dull and lifeless? No, not at all. David is almost purring with delight as he describes what the word of his God is like. David gets personal here: he could be describing a person here. He exclaims it is: *Perfect, Sure, Right, Pure, Clean,* and *True.* What wonderful characteristics. If you were to be described like this wouldn't it be wonderful? But this description could never be properly true of mortal men. How we should treasure this word, what a wonderful gift it truly is. The reason it is so personal is that ultimately it is describing Jesus. Jesus is called the word of God. He is God's final word to mankind. And he has these characteristics.

God's message is relevant

What effect will this word have on us if we take it up and read it? The effects of this word are amazing to behold:

- it will convert my soul,
- it will give me wisdom,
- it will make my heart sing for joy,
- it will enlighten me,
- it will always stay with me,
- it will show what true righteousness is.

It touches every part of my life, my heart and my soul. I dare not travel through life without this guidebook, written by the one who created the very world he has written of. How can I thank God for this precious gift? How should I value it? David praises the words of God like this: *More to be desired are they than gold…by them is your servant warned, and in keeping them is great reward.* If you had a choice would you dine at banqueting hall every night, own a vault full of money, or have the word of God. David knew what he would choose, and he had experienced both. It is what will last for eternity that is worth getting: reading, doing and valuing the word of God above all else is the only way we will get to heaven. This is what we noted in the last chapter. The righteous man follows and obeys this word. Turning aside from the way will only end us in eternal ruin. Riches are great fun for a time, but they have a temporary beauty – a temporary value, which fades away leaving you shrivelled and lost. The Lord Jesus says: *Lay up for yourselves treasures in heaven.*[12]

The response to God's message

The worst thing we can do is to have no response at all. To simply shrug our shoulders at the message of the God of the universe shows us to be unrighteous, and it should be simply unthinkable. David responds in the right way. David's first response is to pray for an <u>honest heart</u>. Having thought

---

[12] Matthew 6 v 20

and written such things, he stops and exclaims: *Who can understand his errors?* It is a rhetorical question that has its own answer. There are simply no errors in God's work or word. However, on the other hand, I do have plenty of errors in both my work and my words. God's word shows them up. It is often a painful book to read for it exposes me. *My heart is deceitful above all things and desperately wicked.*[13] I may not want to see my errors and wrongful ways – in fact I may try to refuse to see them, but God sees them all and records them. David knew something of what his own heart was like, and so he prayed: *Cleanse me from secret faults.*

David also prays for a <u>humble heart</u>. You might think that David, having written such high and mighty praise of God, would be a really holy man. Sometimes Christians laud and honour great preachers both past and present. We have this romantic view that they are more holy than the rest of us. David was aware of thinking this about himself. He asks: *Keep back your servant from presumptuous sins...* Why do you pray for this David? *Then I shall be blameless, and I shall be innocent of the great transgression.* The greatest of men can fall into the greatest of sins, and it can start with becoming presumptuous or complacent. What is the *great transgression?* It refers to the desire to be great in our own eyes – to be like God, to want to have the power over my own

---

[13] Jeremiah 17 v 9

life that God has, and has by creative right. It alludes, perhaps, to the time when Lucifer, son of the morning, originally without sin, said: *I will ascend to heaven... I will be like the Most High,*[14] and we know him as the devil – sentenced to spend eternity in the deepest Hell. Later he was to tempt Eve with the same idea: *You will be like God, knowing good and evil.*[15]It is the oldest temptation in the book, and the most attractive, for it works! We have these desires to be great, greater than we are, or as that famous boxer put it, the greatest! David was aware of this pull, and he prays fervently against it.

David then prays for a <u>right heart.</u> When we consider God: all his majesty, purity and power, it silences the loudest speaker, and humbles the greatest of men. We, like the prophet Isaiah,[16]must set a watch over our lips, and guard what we say, because what we say betrays what we are. David's prayer is beautiful and so profound. *Let the words of my mouth, and the meditation of my heart, be acceptable in your sight O Lord, my strength and my redeemer.* David was called a man after God's own heart. To be in tune with God was his greatest desire, and it should be ours also. Perhaps this verse, at least, should be our daily

---

[14] Isaiah 14 vv 12-14
[15] Genesis 3 v 5
[16] See the story in Isaiah 6 vv 1- 5

prayer as we journey along on the path of life toward the Celestial City.

As we finish this chapter, perhaps it would be a good moment to pause and think and respond to what you have read.

1. Remember what you are picking up: thank God for giving you such a book.
2. Make a commitment to read his book every day.
3. Remember it is a book written to lead you into a relationship with God. Remember the world has one way of looking and understanding things, and God has another. We need the Holy Spirit to be our interpreter so we can understand things in the way God wants us to. That way we shall live in the right way – we shall stay on the right path

The Heavens declare the Glory of God
The skies the work of his hands
Their song is echoed round the world
Their handiwork all through His lands

The skies' strong man rejoices
Exuding, as he runs his race,
God's wisdom, presence and power
Faithfulness, kindness and grace

God's word completes the picture
For his law is all we need
To know, obey and worship
The writer of heavenly creed

As I meditate on your message
In the world, the sky, the sun
I bow, O Strength, my Redeemer
In wonder at all you've done

Chapter 3

The path to the Cross

Please read Psalm 24

In the story of Pilgrim's Progress, Graceless trudges on his journey. On his back he carries this great and heavy burden. This is a picture of what it is like to be burdened with a sense of sin. Graceless is burdened with his sin. He has tried and tried and tried to get rid of it. He has found and lost a friend because of his determination to deal with his sin. He has taken bad advice and been diverted off the path; he has been troubled and been warned of an enemy waiting for him. And yet almost without warning he comes across this amazing place – the only place in the universe – where this burden is dealt with. And did you notice the choice of words I used? He did not loosen the burden, nor did he take it off himself, for he couldn't. At a certain place, it was loosed without him touching it, it came off, it rolled away and - get this – he never saw it again; never. Sin once dealt with is gone forever. Where was this place? It was Calvary. At Calvary there is a cross where a Man died to pay the price for sin. That is why it goes. It rolls into the abyss and dumps itself, as it were, on the head of the father of lies and the author of sin, reminding him of the words spoken to him in the Garden of Eden all those years ago. Graceless was now Christian. He was a free man. He had been redeemed by Jesus' death on that cross, and now having been purchased by the blood of the Son of God; he now belonged to God and would do so for evermore. He was now absolutely sure of his place at the Celestial City, the place the Father and the Son lived. And he cried tears of joy.

What about you? Have you had your sin dealt with by that unseen hand yet, or are you trying to do it yourself? Perhaps you do not think you are a sinner, and what is sin anyway – and who is sin against? Where do we go for eternal life? David asked himself these questions, and when he found the answers he wrote this psalm. First he writes the basic answers as statements; then in poetic style he gives us a picture of the Saviour. It is a great gospel psalm. It gives us the answers to the big questions we ask at one time or another in our lives. The fact is, however, we don't always like the answers.

My Creator

David starts with answering the biggest question of all: *How did I get here?* Related to this is: *Who made me?* Have you asked that question? How did I get here? What is the purpose of my life? Whom do I answer to? The answer to these great and basis questions is both fundamentally important and fundamentally the same, because to answer one is to answer all. If no one made me and I am a random chance happening, as the evolutionist states, then I answer to myself. I live as I like, and I haven't got to worry about a place called heaven because it is not there, and I haven't got to fear hell because it is not there either. What I think counts, and what I do is the only important thing. Everything revolves around me; other people are useful only in terms of how they suit my needs at that particular time. They are at best second in importance to me, and probably in fact not that important at all. Now, you might say that you never think like that, but let's face it, it is the logical end of holding the evolutionist belief and of course deep down it is exactly what we think. Naturally that is how we all think, to varying degrees of selfishness. We are all at heart selfish and self-centred - I am at the centre of my universe; I am the star of my show.

However, if someone made me, then I have a problem to face: there is someone who is far greater than me: there is another star in the show. To that person I am accountable. I would have to ask: *What does my Creator want from me?* I have to find this out. I at the very least have to somehow ensure that I do not displease this Creator because of what he might do to me. Mankind throughout all ages, and in all cultures has shared this fear of the Unknown Creator.[17] This fear has led to a whole host of religious practices based on ignorance and superstition. Diabolical rites, inflicting incalculable suffering on innocent and helpless victims have been carried out over many years – and still are being carried out – in order to appease a supposed offended deity or deities. But God, the Creator, at the beginning of time laid down what He has required, and constantly in history has raised up men to carry on teaching those requirements, adding to the story until the Bible was completed. At that point it became the duty of the church of God to take the word of God – the Bible – and preach it to those who are ignorant of what it teaches. David, then, was in his own day one link in that chain, and here in poetic form answers the big question: who is the Creator? Well we read that, *the earth is the Lord's, and all its fullness, the world and those who dwell therein. For he has founded it upon the seas, and established it upon the waters.* God is the Creator of all things. Think about creation in all its beauty, majesty and detail. Creation declares the glory of God. Creation tells us how marvellous God is, and the Bible is loaded with statements of praise to the creator God. Do not just turn to Genesis to read about God making the world, there are constant references to it throughout the Bible. Think of the **power** that made such a world as this. The words *founded*

---

[17] Think, for example, of what Paul saw at Mars Hill - an altar to the Unknown God.

and *established* literally refer to God setting up, i.e. from nothing, this world. Think about the **wisdom** involved in making such a world with all its variation and interdependence. Think also about the fact that God intimately knows everything about this creation that he has made. What wisdom! It is so far above and beyond what we can even contemplate. Think of the **timelessness** of God. This world has been going for thousands of years, yet God has been in control for every minute of every day of every one of them. He neither slumbers nor sleeps. His years are without end for the Lord reigns forever and ever. What a wonderful God he is.

The holy God

We have seen these facts stated in Psalm 19 in the last chapter. Now David builds on this by asking a very sobering question: *Who may ascend into the hill of the Lord? Or who may stand in his holy place?* Straightaway we find out something about God – He is holy. What does that mean? It means that God is pure: he is without sin and without blemish. He is whiter than new blown snow; more consuming that the hottest fire; cleaner than sparkliest stream, and lighter than the brightest light. God is perfect. Quite clearly, David knows that he is not perfect or pure. He trembles to approach this holy God. In using the words *ascend* and *hill*, David alludes to the time when the people of

Israel were shown something of the awesomeness of God's holiness. It was at Mount Sinai in the desert. Moses went up the mountain to meet God: God came down to the mountain to meet him. The Israelites were terrified at his appearing in cloud and smoke, thunder and lightning, with trumpets sounding.[18] Then this holy, terrifying God showed his Holy Standard. He gave the Ten Commandments. Who indeed would ascend, unbidden, into the hill of the Lord? Not me. Not you either. We would perish instantly. So then, who can go into the presence of this awesome God? *He who has clean hands and a pure heart, who has not lifted up his soul to an idol, nor sworn deceitfully.* The one who can go and meet God must be perfect in his deeds *(he needs clean hands)*, his thoughts *(a pure heart)*, his worship *(he must not have lifted up his soul to a false god)* and in his words *(he must never sworn falsely, told lies or had unclean words flow from his mouth)*. That person will receive blessing, righteousness and salvation (note, by the way, that these things are still gifts) from God. But, I am not perfect and neither are you. We simply cannot go into the presence of God, any more than a tramp covered in filth, muck and reeking enough to make one retch, could wander in welcome in the palace of our own sovereign. That means we are cut off and separated from this wonderful God. Isaiah writes bluntly that: *Your iniquities have separated you from your God, and your sins*

---

[18] Read Exodus Ch. 18 vv 16-18

have hidden his face from you, so that he will not hear.[19] We have a terrible dilemma. An all-powerful God, who is perfect and pure and holy, has made us and although we can see his handiwork, and although we can know lots about him, we cannot know him. When we broke his commandments the very first time we in effect declared war on our own maker. We are at enmity with the Creator God and Lord of the universe! What a terrible, terrible thing.

My Saviour

Strangely, though, the psalm here takes on a completely different note. In fact it seems to be talking about something else altogether. What is all this about gates and doors – and who is this king? David is giving a picture to show that the terrible situation we are in is not the end. Here is the illustration: there is a battle raging. You are under siege and your army is being beaten soundly. You have fought with all your might, but you are beaten, and you sag down exhausted with trying to protect your position, and you cannot fight any longer. The blackness of despair overwhelms you – all is lost. Suddenly, unexpectedly, a trumpet sounds and the gates of your fortress burst open. *Lift up your heads, O you gates, and be lifted up you everlasting doors, and the king of glory shall come in.* You lift

---

[19] Read Isaiah Ch 59 v 2

up your head and gaze in wonder. A king rides in, and what a king is this! He is wearing the most magnificent robes you have ever seen. His face radiates with splendour. There is both joy and gravity on it. You are looking into the face of someone wonderful. Even as you look you feel compelled to get to your knees, and bow to him. He is the king of glory. *Who is this king of Glory? He is the Lord strong and mighty* The words *The Lord* means, Jehovah, or I Am, the self-existing one. This is Jesus, who called himself I Am. This Jesus comes to you and you know the battle is over. You are saved. But, what battle has been fought? It is the battle for your soul. First Jesus has conquered the enemy of your soul – Satan, the devil. Secondly he has solved the problem of your sins – those wrong deeds, words, thoughts and (false) worship. He has taken away the anger of God against you, and God is ready to pardon you. Jesus name means Jehovah Saves, and he has saved you by dying on the cross at Calvary – *the just for the unjust to bring you to God.*[20] He has also dealt with your own obstinacy and rebellion. Perhaps you have fought all your life against God. You have refused to obey his commandments; you have refused to love him and to serve him – your creator. You have fought to the last, but the battle is over. The gates and doors were in fact your own barricades that you set up to defy the Lord. But he has burst them apart. In grace and mercy Jesus comes to you

---

[20] I Peter 3 v 18

and he says: Come to me. I give you these gifts (remember verse 2) of blessing, righteousness and salvation.

My Wonderful Lord

The psalm ends with this note of triumphant praise, and in doing so teaches us that we should praise the one who loved us and gave himself for us. *Lift up your heads, O you gates! Lift up you everlasting doors! And the king of glory shall come in. Who is this king of glory? The Lord of hosts, he is the king of glory.* What remains to be done now? You have to lift up your head and your heart to the king of glory. What does that mean? To carry on with the illustration for a minute – you have to bow to the king and give him the honour that is his due. You personally have to ask and acknowledge him to be your Lord and Saviour, because salvation is an intensely personal thing. The relationship between you and your God is just that – between you and him, and you have to play your part. No one else and nothing else can make you a Christian. You have to ask the Lord for mercy and forgiveness yourself. It is said that on the Battle of Bosworth Field in 1485, that the English lords picked up the crown of England from off a bush and put it on the head of Henry Tudor, and knelt in his presence. He was the king *de facto*; he had won the battle; what remained was for his subjects to recognise the fact of his kingship over them, and that is what they did. You and I must do the same to Jesus Christ: the King of kings and Lord of lords. Crown him your Lord and King. Then you can rightfully belong to his kingdom, which will stand forever. You then are a citizen of Heaven. Notice the kind of awestruck note the psalmist has here. What a wonderful thing it is for Jesus to come into your heart and life, and be there forever.

Have you personally surrendered to Jesus Christ? He is the creator and saviour of the world. He is the one who made you, loved you, lost you, sought you and found you again. Now that you have read this, you also have found him. But that is not enough. Do not read these pages and pass off their message. Ask Jesus Christ to forgive you, save and have mercy on you right now. Don't be a rebel any longer, because when you die, you will be excluded from heaven and spend eternity in hell.

In our story of Pilgrim's Progress remember that Christian came to the Cross at Calvary. There his great burden fell off his back and he saw it no more. Never again was the burden of his sin to be placed on his shoulders. Never again would he stagger and stumble under its weight. No wonder then that we read that he *went on his way rejoicing*.

Now you can do the same.

As I stand at the foot of the Cross
I see a man nailed to the beams
I picture his suffering and pain
His anguish and agony
I know he has done no crime
His executioners all knew it too
He bore his grief alone, cut off
From the friends that he once knew

As I kneel at the foot of the Cross
I hand down my head in shame
For I know I put that man there
And Innocent is really his name
He's there on the Cross for I nailed Him
With my sins to that tortuous tree
He's Jesus Christ, the Righteous One
And he hung and suffered for me

As I fall to the foot of the Cross
I hear him whisper my name
He says: "*Go, you're sins are forgiven
My death means you're born again*"
Now I know I'm his child forever
He's alive and rules over all
And at the foot of the Cross I gave to Him
My life, my heart, my all.

Chapter 4

Sing as you go

Please read Psalm 66

So Christian at Calvary has seen his burden go tumbling. After a while he moves on, to start his road from the Cross to the Celestial City, and we read these words: *he went on his way rejoicing.* Why did he go on his way rejoicing? He was still as poor as ever, still on his own as before, nothing on the outside appeared to have changed at all. Yet one thing had changed: he no longer carried on his back that burden of sin. It had gone. He was a new man recreated from inside by the Holy Spirit of God. He was no longer a lost man but a saved man. He was no longer worried about the wrath to come, for he had a guaranteed entrance to the Celestial City. Bunyan tells us that *three Shining Ones came to him and saluted him with "Peace be to thee"; the second stripped him of his rags and clothed him with change of raiment; the third also set a mark on his forehead and gave him a roll with a seal upon it, which he bade him look on as he ran and that he should give it in at the Celestial Gate"* [21]

---

[21] Ibid. p48

We further read that he gave three leaps for joy and went on singing. I wonder; how did you feel when you were saved? I hope you too rejoiced! What a marvellous thing has happened to you, you have been eternally saved by the Lord Jesus Christ! You have now a new Saviour, friend, master and home. Once you were lost and now you are found. Once you had no hope and no help, and Jesus: the Son of God befriended you. Once you served sin and all ungodliness, now you serve the Lord of heaven and earth. Once you were bound for hell, now you have a guaranteed home in heaven, prepared for you by the Lord himself. No wonder we rejoice! Hallelujah - praise his name! In fact what comes naturally now to us is to worship this crucified Saviour, and now, risen Lord; something we have never wanted to do before. We've started on a joyful career of worship to the Lord of Glory.

But what is worship? How do we worship the Lord? It is something we start when we become a Christian, and it is something we never finish doing. Isn't that a tremendous thought? But what is it? You will soon find if you haven't done so already that Christians differ over how they worship, but should never be differing over the desire and willingness to worship, to borrow Paul's words, the *Son of God who loved me and gave himself for me*[22].

---

[22] Galatians 2 v 20

Christians will worship at various times, in different places, to differing accompaniments, with different people and with differing emphases, and reasons. You will go to one church and find it is completely different from another church. Across the world these differences in style and culture will determine what exactly will go on in each church. The same bible is read, perhaps some of the same hymns will be sung, but there are differences in all sorts of ways. Continually though, there will be this thread running through the lives of the Christians who worship in these churches: they will all have a sense of the in their lives of the "wonderfulness" of God washing over them, both in trouble and in joy. Although worship involves emotion, it is not an emotion. It is first an attitude – a settled decision, that this is something that we will do, and that we want to do - no matter what. It is something that comes from within, and is not dependant on our outward circumstances. We may sing out loud overwhelmed by sheer joy. We may worship in awe after we have seen God at work in an amazing way. We may look up and around us, and sing in sheer wonder at the incredible creation God has made, as we realise afresh how great our God is. And we will worship even in the very worst of times, like Job who after losing all his livestock, his servants and his sons and daughters, *tore his robe* [in grief], *shaved his head; and he fell to the ground and **worshipped**. And he said; 'Naked I came from my mother's womb, and* *naked shall I return there. The Lord gave, and the Lord has taken away; blessed be the name of the Lord.*[23] Worship then, is the reverential act of acknowledging who God is, acknowledging his sovereign right over me and all creation, and humbly giving him the glory, the praise and honour due to himself.

Sometimes our worship is at the very forefront of what we doing, sometimes it is at the back of our minds. But it is there. In this psalm we have this overwhelming sense of praise and joy flowing out of the writer who has been brought face to face with the awesomeness of God.

Before we consider the message of the psalm, there are other things I'd like you to notice. The psalm is anonymous. Some scholars, because of verses 5 – 12, think that Moses wrote it. Some point out that since it is dedicated to the Chief Musician, a title not created until probably David's time, that David himself wrote or commissioned it. Others favour David as author because he dedicated other psalms that he penned to the Chief Musician[24]. It is worth pointing out that in spite of the surrounding psalms 64-69 having similar dedications; Psalm 66 does not ascribe authorship to David. Therefore David is unlikely to be the author. More likely it was penned by one of the choir

---

[23] Job 1 vv 20-21
[24] See, for example, Psalms 4, 5, 6, 8, 9, 11, 64, 65 and 68

of singers in David's time, and if it was, it is encouraging to think that an **ordinary** man is used to compose extraordinary praise, and that an **anonymous** man can leave such an important and wonderful gift for the church. What will you leave the church when you have finished your journey? Perhaps it will be a legacy of saved sinners: perhaps the memory of being a good and faithful parent, teacher or friend, or maybe some other holy work or gift for others to treasure and benefit by.

It's worth a thought isn't it?

We are singing an awesome song

This psalm is dedicated *to the Chief Musician. A song. A psalm.* This is a psalm, and this is a song. It would be worthwhile just to pause here and think about this. Firstly notice the word *Selah.* This is a musical term meaning pause, and as it is part of the song's structure we should do that. Selah tells us that we should think about what we sing. Then notice the dedication to the Chief Musician. Sometimes the psalmist set his own tune[25], at others he would stipulate what instruments were to be used,[26] but here the writer gives it to the Chief Musician to compose the tune. He has

[25] See, for example, Psalms 45, 53 and 60
[26] See, for example, Psalms 61, 67 and 76

the scope to compose and arrange as he sees fit before God.

Now, why mention all this? Some Christians are very specific about what music is sung or what instruments can be used, and they choose from a very small range; others have a broader range of either or both. This often is a contentious issue in the church, but an issue we must look at with an open and honest mind. Go through the psalms and see for yourself the variety of music, styles, themes and purposes that is in this holy psalter, and ask how biblical are we in our worship? What is biblical worship? Is it a set pattern of service? Is it only a certain instrument? Is it anything you like with anyone you like? Is the same thing right all the time? Is worship more or most spiritual because of these things? I ask the questions that you may ask them of yourself, and come to a biblical answer. And you may be certain of one thing: because the Lord has made us different we will come to a certain extent to differing conclusions.

We at all times must be reverent in all we do, for we worship a holy God. We are worshipping, not performing. Variety does not mean license to frivolity or thoughtlessness – anything will not do. The very pointed lesson I am bringing out here is that we must give very careful thought and prayer to how we worship this awesome God.

An Awesome God

This song bursts into life: *Make a joyful shout to God, all the earth!* I am an Englishman, and we English are often noted for our reserve. When was the last time I shouted to God for joy? This verse takes me out of my comfort zone. What is it telling me to do? It is saying as a citizen of the world I should praise God openly, loudly and with all my heart – nothing less will do. The word *shout* means to uproar, and the word *joyful* means to shout for joy. You see the double emphasis here? God's created people are to make a "shout for joy uproar". That does not diminish one iota the reverence we show to the Lord, but it does emphasise the natural response of joy we should have to him. *Sing out the honour of his name; make his praise glorious.* This is the least I can do to the one who made me. *Say to God, 'How are awesome are your works! Through the greatness of power your enemies shall submit themselves to you. All the earth shall worship you and sing praises to you; they shall sing praises to your name'.* God is awesome in creation. This theme is tirelessly sung throughout the psalms, and it is one we should never tire of. I heard a preacher once say: "If you believe Genesis 1 v 1 then believing the rest of the bible is easy!" When we remember that our God is the God of creation, we much more easily remember that he is also the God of providence, time, order and eternity, and then we are far more ready to come to him in faith, in reverence and in awe. Just because our God is our wonderful heavenly Father, that does not mean we forget to come to him in the right way – the reverent way. We may certainly come with boldness, but never carelessness, insolence or indifference.

It won't end with praising God for his wonderful creation however. There are even greater songs to sing: songs of salvation; of redemption, of eternal life! We should sing many songs to God, and not just in church. Paul wrote of *singing and making melody in your heart to the Lord.* God's people should be a singing people. God's people should compose spiritual songs to God, dedicating them to the one who loved us and gave himself for us. God's people should be a joyful people. Even when our life is hard, we should still sing to God because God's love never changes; our salvation never diminishes and our Lord Jesus is still preparing our eternal home for us. The greatness of our salvation is not reliant on how we feel, but upon God's solemn promises, and so should our worship be.

Selah: pause; reflect; marvel. If you and I did this one thing each day: paused, reflected and marvelled on the greatness of our God, we would live changed lives. We would see the big picture that this psalmist saw: we would be led to complain less, be less petty in our thinking and instead to trust and praise God more. Now how much good would that do to our own lives, and to the effectiveness of our witness to the Lord Jesus in the world? Our testimony would be more and more: *Come and see the works of God; he is awesome in his doing towards the sons of men.*

Awesome in history

Israel was a little state. There were always those who would scoff at her and question her very reason for existence. Plenty of times her enemies tried to wipe her out. The first major power was Egypt. They tried to strangle the nation even before it was born. When Moses led the people of Israel out of Egypt Pharoah pursued them to the great river. What could Israel do? They were helpless, but God *turned the sea into dry land; they went through the river on foot.* The Egyptians were overthrown. Here is their history lesson. What was the lesson to be learned from this? *We will rejoice in him.* Why? *He rules by his power forever; his eyes observe the nations; [so] do not let the rebellious exalt themselves.* Again and again in the bible we have this history lesson brought up. It is the seminal point – the fulcrum on which the very existence of the nation of Israel turned. If the deliverance had not happened, then there would be no Israel. God, to show once and for all his commitment, his love and his choosing of Israel to be his people, constantly turns their minds to this event: "what more evidence of my love and compassion to you could you ever ask for", he in effect says. And so, the Israelites could always turn their minds back to that first great deliverance and remind themselves both of God's goodness and greatness, and encourage themselves with his faithfulness in whatever situation they found themselves in. It is the same for us. Our first great deliverance was at the cross so, if God gave up his Son for us *how then shall he not with him freely give us all things?* [27] We can be sure that God will provide for us on our journey, as he has done for his children in the past.

Selah; pause, reflect and marvel on how God has worked in your life in the past, and remember that you have been given the Holy Spirit as a deposit guaranteeing your future with him.

Awesome in patience and purpose

Although we have these history lessons to guard and guide us we do so often forget them. Nevertheless God never lets us go even though we stray (see chapter 9), *Oh bless our God you peoples! And make the voice of his praise to be heard; who keeps our soul among the living, and does not allow our feet to be moved.* The picture here given is that of a world stage where we watch nation after nation and Satanic scheme after scheme rise against God's people,

---

[27] Romans Ch. 8 v 32

threaten, appear triumphant and then fall and fail, and we are exhorted to praise the omnipotent God who controls all things and who does all things well. It also could be that *peoples* refer to successive generations of God's people, so that there is a never-ending chorus of praise to God for his protection of his people. God has a great purpose through all circumstances to preserve his people until the day of his coming again to take them home. Though we often wander, the Lord never lets us go, and though we are opposed, we never are struck down. God is patient with us, tender, as he knows our weakness, he remembers we are but dust. We will never be plucked from our Father's hand. He does not allow it and he is strong enough to prevent it.

However there is a more positive aspect to God's purpose and patience. God has a plan for his church, and that means a plan for you. How awesome is that! There are things he wants you to do, places he wants you to go, deeds he wants you to accomplish, a standard of holiness he wants you to fight to live by, and a life he wants you to glorify him with. That is the biggest and best life plan of all, and no matter how old, young, gifted or ordinary you were when you were saved, God is going to take you and use you for his glory. That is **awesome!** How incredible that God is that interested in us; that he would bother to give us anything to do for him, when with just a word he could accomplish all things by himself. He allows us into his plans, purposes and work. This both humbles us to the lowest place to think we can do nothing of ourselves, and yet elevates us to the highest court of all, when we think the king of kings and lord of lords appoints us as his ambassadors. Sounds easy, doesn't it? It isn't. What it does mean is that we are disciples, and that means we are under authority and discipline of the Holy Spirit. Look at these words: *For you, O God, have tested us; you have refined us as silver is refined. You brought us into the net: you laid affliction on our backs. You have caused men to ride over our heads; we went through fire and water, but you brought us out to rich fulfilment.* This reads almost like a commentary on Hebrews 12 vv 5-11, especially on the phrase in verse 11: *no chastening seems to be joyful... but painful; nevertheless afterward it yields the peaceable fruit of righteousness for those who have been trained by it.* In life to get a skill we have to train. Training is often tough, arduous and seemingly pointless. But at the end of it all you look back and see why you did those things and know their lasting benefit. How much more in the training college of God where we learn and train for spiritual qualities? The choice of the words *fire and water* teach us that God's testing is to purify us and separate us from the world, to stop us wandering back to where we came from. Jesus wants us to be like him, so how much have we learned in that college? When we look back after a period of time in our Christian walk we should see we have learned. The psalmist clearly had, for he exclaims: *I will go into your house with burnt offerings; I will pay you my vows which my lips have uttered and my mouth has spoken when I was in trouble.*

Selah; pause, reflect and marvel on what God is doing with your life and in your life. Review it regularly. How far have you come on in your Christian life? What are you doing for God – what are you being for God? We should not get too introspective – but regular reflection is good practice to ensure we are still on the right path, and to check we are more and more ready for the heavenly home and company we shall possess. David's prayer: *Search me O God* [28]should be a regular part of our praying to him who sees all. Commit your life to the Lord anew asking the Lord to accomplish his will in your life more and more.

Awesome in mercy

Come and hear, all you who fear God, and I will declare what he has done for my soul. I cried to him with my mouth, and he was extolled with my tongue. The psalm finishes on a great note of thanks to God. The psalmist still wants to sing out loud to God; he still wants others to join the song of praise to God for all his goodness and mercy. How awesome is that mercy which means God listens to people like us and that he accepts and delights in our heartfelt praise. It is awesome that God, who is worshipped

---

[28] Psalm 139 v 1

by angelic beings (whose majestic splendour would cause us to tremble), is interested in my praise. What mercy, what condescension, is there in this – such knowledge is too wonderful for me, it is too high for us to understand.

Yet there is one condition to all our worship being acceptable to God: it must be offered honestly. Look at verse 18: *If I regard iniquity in my heart the Lord will not hear. But certainly God has heard me; he has attended to the voice of my prayer.* How terrible a thing it would be for me to pray whilst hiding sin in my heart – in other words knowing I had or was doing wrong things, or harbouring wrong thoughts and yet I pray to God as if nothing was wrong. What good is it pretending that the all-seeing one cannot see into my heart? Yet we've all done it haven't we? God does not listen to a prayer like this. Deal with your sin first and then when your fellowship is restored, go on to your praise and petitions. In all things, and at all times be honest with God. It is the most crucial thing in any relationship with any person – how much more then is it for you as a Christian?

Thanks

Blessed be God, who has not turned away my prayer, nor his mercy from me! Listen to this last note of utter triumph, thankfulness and love. How good God is to me. How much I should praise him. How much should I serve him? You truly are an awesome, Lord. Hang on to that fact as you continue on your way - rejoicing!

Lord I sing in awe and wonder
At the marvellous things you've made
'Gainst your enemies you shall thunder
They will see your power displayed
All the earth will sing your praises
They'll submit themselves to you
As they look with awe-struck gazes
At the marvellous things you do

Israel were once kept in bondage
Till released at your command
They were trapped beside the river
Till you turned sea to dry land
There they went on foot to Canaan
Safe and sound from all their foes
By your power you rule forever
Your eyes still watch the nations go

Bless Jehovah all you peoples
Make his praise heard far and wide
For this God preserves his loved ones
Though like silver they are tried
Cruel men lash their affliction
Choke with water, burn with fire
Though the Lord permits refining
Divine love will never tire

Come and hear all you God-fearers

What the Lord has done for me

My heart must be truly honest

It must shun iniquity

But the Lord has certainly listened

He did hear this servant's prayer

Blessed be God whose awesome kindness

Will surround me everywhere

Chapter 5

It's a difficult road at times

Please read Psalm 91

Christian, then, went *on his way rejoicing.* What happened next to him? Did he have a great time of uninterrupted joy and happiness? The greatest thing in his life had just burst on his soul. It was not, however, a happy ever after, but a conflict just beginning. He is walking the road that leads to the Celestial City. He is determined to get there. The Lord of the Celestial City is equally determined to protect and help him on his journey, and he has all the means necessary to do this. The Shining Ones have provided Christian with some helps. But Christian also now has an enemy who is determined to frustrate, discourage and turn him aside from his course. We shall see this as we follow the story. After he left the cross and went on his way, Christian encountered fairly early on a variety of difficulties, put for us in the shape of men:

• He encounters apathy – Three men called Simple, Sloth and Presumption are chained but asleep, oblivious of the danger of judgement and Hell they are in and the cure of the cross.

- He encounters scorn – Two men called Formalist and Hypocrisy tell him the cross is nothing special and in fact that it is too hard a way, and if Christian has got any sense he'll use their shortcuts and save himself a lot of trouble. When he insists that his way is right and theirs is wrong they laugh at him and tell him there are plenty of other ways into the Celestial City.

- He encounters Difficulty, in this case having to go up a steep hill alone, which reduces him from running [with joy], to walking to clambering on his hands and knees.

- He encounters faintheartedness. He meets Timorous and Mistrust - people to try to make him give up and go back. They tell him that there are lions in the way which will certainly devour him, and the only sensible thing to do is to turn around and go back.

You will encounter all these situations – Fact. All Christians do. In Britain, we have apathy all around us. People don't care what you believe, or what anyone else believes as long as you let them get on with their lives. Eternity is just unimportant. Apathy is the hardest thing to pierce. It is as if a person is in a stupor, what can you do to wake them up? Other people do not like what they see as the restrictiveness of Christianity and they tell us there are plenty of other ways which are not as hard as ours that lead to heaven. Sometimes life as a Christian is plain hard, and we are tempted to have a break from it all, and rest from serving God. The trouble is if we do that we seldom get going again. Sometimes it is frightening being a Christian and we are tempted to worry about what is going to happen to us. What should we do in all these things? We must cry out to God for protection. Will God protect us? This psalm shows that that he will, it was written to comfort the pilgrims of years ago to tell them that God would protect them. It tells us who is protecting us, from what and why.

Who wrote this psalm? It is anonymous, but Spurgeon makes the point that there is a tradition amongst Hebrew scholars that if an anonymous psalm follows a named one, then the author of the previous psalm is likely to be the author of that one also. This being the case, the author would be Moses.

Whoever wrote it must have had Deuteronomy and the theme of pilgrimage in mind. I think that Moses may well have written it. He was an eloquent writer (cf. Psalm 90) even if he did not count himself as an eloquent speaker. Deuteronomy 32 and 33, which were written by him, certainly are worthy of psalm-like status.

Another thing to mention, in addition the fact that there is no stated author, is that there are no other inscriptions either. There is no title; no direct purpose (i.e.

Song for the Sabbath Day); no music set, and no dedication. Only 33 of the 150 psalms are like this. They are universal psalms, for all God's people at all times.

The Christian's safety

The psalm starts off, as many do, with a great declaration; *He who dwells under the secret places of the Most High* (Elyon), *shall abide under the shadow of the Almighty* (Shaddai).These two names of God give us a great of understanding of him. First, he is God Most High *(Elyon)*. He is the God who is high and lifted up with his train filling the temple that Isaiah gasped in awe and wonder at. Yet he is also *Shaddai*, the root of the word comes from *shad*, which means breast[29], according to Scroggie, denoting mother-protection. At once we are introduced to two strikingly different pictures of God: the omnipotent God, and the comforting protector. This is a great comfort to us pilgrims on the way. We have no home, yet we dwell in secret place of God most high – the greatest, most powerful being in existence, the one who creates by his word, and sustains all things. We may feel alone as the pilgrim in the story, yet we are under the shadow of the Almighty protector, the one of whom it is said, he that touches you touches the apple of his eye. The Lord is our refuge and fortress. We might think of castles and strongholds here but it could also be true of

---

[29] Psalms Volume 2, p. 250

the Passover night. In that night the children of Israel were in a safe place, and under the shadow of the protection of God. He had given them a refuge to run to from the Angel of Death, as we have Christ, and they that took advantage of it were safe. A house so protected was a fortress and refuge from disaster. Although disaster strikes it will not deflect us from our calling any more than it deflected Israel from getting (eventually) to Canaan.

The Christian's Dangers

How can I be in danger and safe at the same time? There is, as we have already seen, danger for the Christian. What danger? In verse 3 we have the danger of the crafty trapper. Here is a man or woman (and of course we have to see the devil that old enemy of souls at work behind the scenes), who for whatever reason wants to trap the Christian. They will have their own reasons: perhaps it is the pleasure of seeing a good person ruined such as Delilah ruining Samson, or Potiphar's wife trying to ruin Joseph. It could be the pricking conscience such as Ahab who said of the prophet Micaiah that he hated them because he told the truth and he didn't want to hear it as it always spoiled his fun. Such truth contradicts the way these people want to live their lives even though they know their way is wrong. It is perverse but all too common (1 Kings 22 v 8). Or it could be pride such as the Pharisees, Sadducees and scribes had in trying to trick and entangle the Lord Jesus, so that they could discredit him, and once again look the top teachers in Israel. All sorts of motives, and all sorts of ways of carrying out those motives but beware, there are some people who will try and trap you and ruin your witness, and walk with the Lord.

Another danger (v3) is that of perilous pestilence. Who or what is the pest here? The Authorised Version has it as noisome pestilence. *Noisome* translates as rushing: falling upon, there is a sense of eagerness and you get the picture of one army rushing towards a hapless victim and tearing it apart in blood lust. *Pestilence* translates as destroying like a plague. Two very strong words are used to show that there is great enmity against the Christian. Later in the story Christian encounters Apollyon – the captain of the satanic guard who, so enraged that the pilgrim had changed sides to follow the Lord, fell upon him in fury and tried to finish him off there and then. Satan wants to rush upon us with the same wrath and do away with us. He may fling disease, opposition or enmity upon us in order to knock us off the journey we are embarked on. Sometimes those terrors are at night (v5): sometimes they are attacks like arrows in broad daylight (v6). Think of the fury of Haman on Mordecai, which then led to him hatching a plot to destroy all the Jews, or Sennacherib on Hezekiah's Judah: Saul on David. What is the danger here? Well if the first danger has the air of subtlety about it, the second method used against us is just the opposite. It is full frontal assault. It is fierce. It is frightening. Have you ever been afraid to be a Christian? That is when this sort of attack comes against you.

Since it is a stated Bible fact that no Christian can fall away and be lost (or killed to pursue the metaphor), how can we understand v 7? It exposes us to another danger: discouragement when we see how tough the fight is, and particularly when we see professing Christians fall away. Not every who begins finishes the race – only those who are the real competitors. Some seem to begin well and then they fall. What about us: will we fall away from the one who loved us and gave himself for us? It is not possible. Just because the enemy has stopped them from being saved, he cannot stop you. Those who try to stop your pilgrimage, and those who give up will be dealt with and you will see it with your own eyes.

So, to sum up these dangers, they are manifold. They are real. They are carefully designed by the enemy to stop you, to ruin your walk with God and your witness for him. The title of John Newton's biography is: Through many dangers. Remember the word: "through" There are many dangers, but the Lord will protect us from each one. Look at the words here that show what God is doing to protect you. If you dwell, abide, in him, then he is your fortress, shield and

buckler. He will deliver, cover, and give refuge to you. C. H.
Spurgeon quotes two people on this: Charles Bradley wrote:
*It is a security in the very midst of evils. Not like the
security of angels - safety in a world of safety, quiet in a
calm; but it is quiet in a storm, safety amid desolation and
the elements of destruction, deliverance where everything
else is going to wreck.*[30] Thomas Watson added; *God doth not
say no afflictions shall befall us, but no evil.* [31]

The Christian's Protector

So we are in danger, but we are safe at the same
time: this is because God sends us protection. Firstly we are
protected by Promise. Look at verse 9. Because you have
taken refuge in him, and have made the most High your
dwelling place, you can count on his protection. Look at it this
way. You have become a citizen of Heaven, and the king of
Heaven has promised that he will look after his citizens. It
would be unthinkable, wouldn't it, that this king is fickle or
inept. He never breaks his promises for he never changes his
mind: he is never unable to complete what he starts. And so
he is able to fulfil this promise, and he does so because he
loves you.

---

[30] C. H. Spurgeon: Treasury of David, Vol. 2 part 2 page 104
[31] op. cit. page 104

You are protected by <u>Angels.</u> God sends his own heavenly soldiers to protect you. This is not the time to divert to a study of angels, but the text says quite plainly that angels are real, that they are active and that they are on duty looking after you. Have a look at Genesis 19 v 15; 2 Kings 6 v 17; Daniel 6 v 22; Matthew 4 v 11. As we are God's fellow workers in the natural world, so they are in the spiritual. Isn't it a wonderful thought that the angels are escorting us on our pilgrimage, on our journey to Heaven?

And we are protected from <u>Satan.</u> In v 13, two interesting pictures for that which could harm us are given: the lion and the poisonous serpent. It is reasonable to take this as two pictures of the devil, since the New Testament does. John calls Satan that *ancient serpent* who deceived Eve,[32] and Peter calls Satan a *roaring lion who goes around seeking whom he may devour.*[33] Even in this phrase: *"may devour"*, is the implication that the devil can only devour those he is permitted. Notice again the twin strategy of attack; the sneaky, subtle but deadly snare, and the aggressive, front-on intimidating all out assault. What shall we do to this enemy? We shall trample him underfoot, but not because we are stronger than the devil, but because the Lord Jesus is, and he will protect us from him as long as we

---

[32] Revelation Ch. 12 v 9 and 20 v 2
[33] I Peter 5 v 8

keep close to him. And we have this assurance: *The God of peace shall crush Satan under your feet shortly.*[34]

We are also protected by God's response to our devotional praying. Look at verses 14 and 15. This protection is not something mechanical. It is something relational. God and his pilgrim are joined together by love and prayer. See how the prayer and response are juxtaposed:

We have set our love upon him, we read in verse 14:

John writes (1 John 4 verse 10): *We love him because he first loved us.*

I will set him on high, says v 14:

Revelation 22 v 5 says, *and they shall reign with me for ever and ever.*

You shall call and he will answer, says v 15:

Ask and you shall be given, said the Lord Jesus (Matthew 7 verse 7).

There is this relationship between the Christian and the Lord that is so intimate, so personal, and this is the source of all these promises, all this safety and all this protection. I challenge you to examine your relationship with the Lord. Is it mechanical? Do you do certain things, fulfil certain duties and plod on regardless? Is your relationship based on habit or is it real: is it personal? When you pray, do you say a prayer or do you talk to a friend that you know: a holy awesome friend, but one who delights to hear you. John

---

[34] Romans 16 v 20

White wrote: *remember he seeks you and longs to speak with you.*[35] On Wednesday 23rd September 1857, Samuel Prime records[36], six men went to a noon-day prayer meeting in a 3rd floor lecture room in New York. It wasn't organized by a mission or church but by a lone missionary who ached inside for God to save the lost thousands in New York. Within two years revival came, not only in New York but all over North America. The publishers of the book called it "the event of the century." What was different about what they did? Thousands of people go to prayer meetings don't they? The difference was they went to pray out of a sense of desperation and prayed and pleaded with their God to save lost souls in the city. The difference was that they were not going to a prayer meeting at all. They were going to pray; and pray their hearts out. They were for real, their prayers were for real, and so were God's answers. Do I pray like this? Do you? This prayer of Moses in vv 14-15 is real praying; there is no sense of formality or hypocrisy or humdrum, boring, ritualistic, habitual prayer. It is real communication; there is an honesty in it all. We must pray like this. We must have a relationship with God like this.

The Christian's blessed assurance

---

[35] The Fight p.26
[36] The Power of Prayer p.8

We have the protector's assurance in the last verse of long life and salvation. Long life to the ancient Israelite, meant a sign of God's blessing. We know that long life – not on earth particularly – but in heaven is a result of that blessing: long life for the Christian is eternal life. What could be better than that? Salvation is spiritual safety; we shall reign with him forever and ever. Can you think of anything more wonderful? We shall be satisfied then with all the best that God can give us. Truly we do well to meditate on these things. Allow these things to encourage you on your pilgrimage: think about how much God has in store for you when he calls you home. In the meantime as we've noted before, he has places for you to go, work for you to do and a message for you to take to those who are lost and bound for hell. That message is the word of life, which you have embraced and which has set you on the road to heaven. To borrow from John Newton's hymn: remember this as you journey on your way through many dangers, toils and snares. It is God's grace that has brought you safe up 'til now, and it is God's grace that will take you safely home. Moses said: *The eternal God is your refuge, and underneath* [you] *are the everlasting arms* (Deut 33 v 27).

The Church's blessed assurance

The psalm was written not just for one individual, it was also a national psalm, written for the nation of Israel.

God's people have this assurance as a body of people, for they are all his people. We, the church universal, have this assurance for Christ Jesus will build his church and the gates of hell will not prevail against it. The church will be here ready and waiting like a bride when Jesus Christ comes to claim her, despite all the dangers, pestilences and arrows of hate that can and are thrown against it, and the traps so wickedly lain to nullify its witness, power and testimony to the Lord Jesus Christ - he who loved her and gave himself for her. Remember, as you live out your life in a society that appears to have turned its back on God, and as you serve in a church which appears to be so small and weak: it isn't the first time in church history it has appeared to be thus, and it probably (if the Lord tarries) won't be the last. But God doesn't change: he is the one who does the changing. Again and again in history God has revived his church, made it a great force for good in the world and brought countless thousands to a personal faith in him. No matter how bad it looks, revival is but one answered prayer away. Although the church as a whole and you as an individual are constantly under enemy attack, yet the Lord will not be thwarted: he will build his church and bring it through all these things to be a glorious, beautiful and magnificent church on the Last Day and forevermore.

My song shall be of God most high
And his protecting power
He surrounds you like a wall
Protects you like a tower

From fowler's snare and pestilence
The Lord shall keep you safe
With softest wings He'll cover you
You need not be afraid.

Thousands may fall at your right hand
It seems you'll perish too
You'll gaze amazed at the wicked's fate
It won't come near to you

Your God by choice your refuge is
In plague you shall be calm
For angel eyes o'er you keep watch
Their hands prevent your harm

The lion's and the cobra's head,
You'll trample underfoot
"Set your love on me," says God
And I will do you good".

So for you O Christian pilgrim
God sets you up on high
And as you walk he guards and keeps
And will always satisfy.

Chapter 6

Let's have a Rest

Please read Psalm 84

Last time we left Christian climbing the hill of Difficulty. After an adventure or two he was very tired and weary. Then he saw in the distance a wonderful building. Its name was Beautiful. It was a house built by the Lord of the Hill to refresh weary pilgrims. A porter opens the door and welcomes him in. He meets other citizens of heaven there and is fed and refreshed in this place. He shares his story so far along the journey with them. He sleeps in a chamber called Peace. He rises and is shown the ancient stories that the Lord of that House had written down, of great pilgrims who had gone before. In this house in fact he is taught many things: given a glimpse of Heaven, but then on the final day he leaves with a suit of armour which he will need for the next phase of his journey. What a house! Do we Christians have a house like this, built by the Lord? Yes we do, and we find out about in this lovely psalm.

This psalm is all about the house of God, and the pilgrim's desire to be in it, and why he longs for it so. It fits our picture so well of the Christian as a pilgrim journeying on his way. As we journey through life we have all kinds of things happen to us. One of the greatest things are those times when we as weary and thirsty and tired pilgrims come to the place of refreshment from those wearying Valley of Baca places, and are refreshed for the next step of the way.

First things first

It is important to look at the information we are given before the psalm begins, because it all helps us understand what we are reading. It is addressed to the *Chief Musician.* We have seen this phrase before. Who was he? King David gave the whole worship of God a real structure when he appointed certain people to lead and organise the worship of God.[37] He recognised the prophets and appointed musicians, singers and arrangers. He also appointed chiefs of all these divisions of servants: Asaph, Heman and Jeduthun. The most well known was Asaph, who clearly was a wonderful man, much loved by the people, for Nehemiah honours his memory by mentioning him alongside David some 500 years later.[38] Although he was a psalm writer, and mainly a teacher, he did not write this psalm, but perhaps he was the one who set it to music.

This psalm also has another pre-script: *upon an instrument of Gath.* Some take it to be a musical term either

---

[37] See I Chronicles Ch. 16 vv 4-6,37; 23 v 5; 25 vv 1-6
[38] See Nehemiah Ch. 12 v 46

denoting the instrument – in particular a harp, or the tune, namely a Gittite tune, and that this tune was a march, and if used on route to the temple, then literally a march to Zion! We could discuss this at length comparing it to the other two psalms with this term, but the point is that it shows again how thoughtfully planned the worship of God was in David's time. Here is another example we should carefully notice that the writer of this psalm gave very careful balanced attention to the worship of God.

The last part of the pre-script is also very interesting: *of* [or for] *the sons of Korah.* Korah was a Levite; a descendent of Kohath. This Kohath was a contemporary of Moses and Aaron, but did not like the fact that they were in charge. He rebelled and so did some of the Reubenites, who no doubt felt that as the sons of the eldest tribe they should be in charge of the people of Israel. These rebels were swallowed up by an earthquake, and died. However, and this is the point, Korah's sons did not die. Therefore the *sons of Korah* were those who were spared, even though children of disobedient parents were invariably sentenced to death alongside their parents[39]. These obtained mercy and grace. To dedicate this psalm to the sons of Korah seems to me to dedicate it to all those who have known God's grace: if it was written by the sons of

---

[39] See for example Achan, and the enemies of Daniel who put him in the lion's den.

Korah, then those recipients of grace are those who are quick to praise the God of all mercy. The sons of Korah were in time appointed by God to be singers, bakers of shewbread and doorkeepers for the Tabernacle, and any of these occupations that the writer had would have been a perfect foil to write this psalm. God uses our gifts, and our knowledge and our place in life to his glory, and so he has here in a wonderful way, for there are few psalms as lovely as this. As Levites, the sons of Korah would have had no possessions, or inheritance; their portion was the service of God. This writer at least was showing that he was more than happy with God had given him and appointed him to be. That is a good lesson for us.

The pilgrim's longing for the house of God

How lovely is your tabernacle. God's house is well-beloved. It is precious and dear to the psalmist. Why? No doubt that although the tabernacle was old by this time and soon to be replaced in the reign of the next king by a temple, it stirred up great feelings in the psalmist. It had been beautifully, carefully and skilfully made, with finest materials, and to a heavenly prototype.[40] This was a place designed by God, commissioned by God, and to be used for the worship of God. No wonder it was precious. The psalmist calls God *O Lord of Hosts.* This term translates as: Jehovah

---

[40] See Exodus 26 v 30

of the masses, which can have a military connotation. In other words God is over all men, but in particular he is the leader and commander of his own special army; the people of God. The surrounding nations had their local deities, all false and worthless but this pilgrim was going to meet with the Lord of all.

My soul longs, yes even faints for the courts of the Lord; my heart and my flesh cry out for the living God. There is such strong feeling here. The words are literally denoting a pining away. Is he not going over the top? To our experience, perhaps he is, but this man loves the courts of God. He loves the people of God who are there. He loves everything about the place. To be away, and we assume he must be, is a terrible thing for him. He is even jealous of the birds that unthinkingly make their home there. How he would love to be sharing in the blessing of those who are. They were praising, and he wishes that he were too.

Selah. Pause, reflect and marvel on the privileges of being in God's house. Is that how we feel about getting there?

The pilgrim struggles to get to the house of God

For this man on his way back to the tabernacle the way was very hard. There were many trials. This is true for all pilgrims everywhere. The man who determines to get to the house of God, whether it be the thrice-yearly pilgrimage to Jerusalem, or on his way back there after being kept away (some writers think this speaks of David in his flight from Absalom), was going to need the Lord's strength to get there. He can be assured of that help though (verse 5), but on this pilgrimage there will hard times, tough times and sad times. This is pictured for us here in verse 6, where an image well-known to Davidic Israelites talks of a certain valley. In this valley, called Baca, were a cluster of trees; some say mulberry, others, more convincingly, Balsam. These trees would shed tears of gum and were known as weeping trees. This then is a weeping valley, we might say, a vale of tears, or (to borrow from psalm 23) a valley of the shadow of death. The meaning is clear: to get to God's house here on earth and to heaven afterward requires us to go through the valley of tears – lots of tears, for they form into pools. We shed tears on our journey through life don't we? David asked God to *put my tears into your bottle.*[41] If we were to pour them all out they would make pools and streams. And those streams of sorrow *go from strength to strength; each one appears before God in Zion.* Yet in those times he must keep going, calling upon God to hear his prayer for help.

Selah. Pause, reflect and marvel on the sorrows of your own pilgrimage. Can you see how God has helped you through it? Can you see that it has strengthened your desire to keep close to God?

---

[41] Psalm 56 v 8

The house of God was the only place to be

For a day in your courts is better than a thousand. I would rather be a doorkeeper in the house of my God, than to dwell in the tents of wickedness. The extremity of thought is striking: one day here rather than three years there. How many places can you think of where that would be true of you? No contest says the psalmist, and what's more I don't even want the best seat in the house. I am happy to be a doorkeeper, just right on the fringe, barely in, scarcely noticed. This man, don't forget, knew what he was he was talking about - either he or his cousins were actually doorkeepers! Rather than dance with the wicked (the word "dwell" means to gyrate!), he would rather be at peace in God's house. *The Lord God is a sun and a shield:* a fitting image for the pilgrim: the sun to keep him warm, and the shield to protect him from enemies – natural or human. Furthermore, *the Lord will give grace and glory,* grace to save and glory everlastingly in heaven. The Lord will see to it; he is looking after each of his journeying children, guarding and guiding us until we reach the Celestial City. There are wonderful prospects for the man who trusts in you, exclaims the psalmist. This word "trust" is worth noting. It means to hail for refuge. Think about that image. Here is one who is strong enough to keep me safe, and who promises he will. I just need to call out to him and he will come. There simply is no better place than the court of God here and no better place than the place it prefigures – heaven.

What do you think of the house of God?

But, how do we view the house of God? We may not be all that wrapped up in the building, although we have a duty to keep it as well as we can because it is the place we have set apart to worship God in, to meet together and to be instructed. We may not enjoy the preacher's style or the hymn book or a host of other things. But going to the house of God is not just about going to a building, performing a religious ritual and going home again. It is about meeting with God's people for God's people collectively are the building – they are the temple, the house of God. It is inconceivable that the psalmist would have wanted just to go the tabernacle on his own. He would have wanted to praise God with God's people. Christ told us he is building his church, and that church is his blood-bought people. They are precious to him, and so they should be to us. As a Christian you should have a spiritual affinity with God's people for they are also your people, and they will be so eternally. There should be a desire within you to want to be with God's people, worshipping God together, singing his praise in unison of voice and heart. Although we are on a journey, we do not always travel alone. God has placed us together in local spiritual families to help and encourage one another on the way. Satan tries at every turn to divide us and stop us walking together. We must be aware of his schemes and strive to keep the unity of the spirit in the bond of peace. See, says the Lord, that you love one another.

However this is all too hard to do if we do not actually go to the house of God. We must go every time God's people meet to worship and be taught. Listen again to the psalmist's eagerness to be at the place of worship. Is yours and mine the same as his? Do we skip off; make excuses, feign illnesses? Let's be honest, we all have times when we don't want to go, but recognise that at that time you probably most need to go. Be faithful to him who was faithful unto death for us: go and worship him who is worthy of all your worship and all your praise. After Christian had left the Beautiful house, he was well equipped for the next part of the journey.

Something to think about

There are many practical lessons to come from this psalm. I will just put them down here for you to think about. Be honest as you do- it could change your life!

- Compare what the psalmist thought as important with your own values in life. How much time, adoration, attention, money, thinking and conversation do the local petty deities take up of your life?

- Think about your order of service. Why do you have it like that? Is it mere custom, or is as a result of careful, prayerful planning. How have you ensured that God is honoured, reverenced and worshipped in a way he is pleased with?

- Think about the journey to church. Are we faithful? Can the fellowship bank on us being there, Sunday morning and evening? What about the prayer meeting? Will nothing – not even life's vales of tears, keep us away?

- When we come, and when we have left, above everything else we have done let us make sure we have worshipped God with all our heart, soul, mind, and strength, for if we cannot do it in the house of God, where else can we do it? The Lord deserves the best we can give him. Let us make sure we give it to him in his own house.

Tired and weary; the way is tough to keep

I see a sight that makes my spirit leap

Upon the hill a lovely building spy

The lord has built it - saints to satisfy

Blessed are they Lord who in your house can dwell

Even the nesting birds your praises tell

So, how much more should I be there to sing

I long for you my God, my Lord, my King

Pilgrimage is hard: the Baca valley's tears

Oft are my portion journeying through the years

Yet you my Lord count up every one

And you protect me with your Shield and Sun

A day in your house is worth thousands elsewhere

Give me the choice I always would be there

Even at the door – it is enough for me

For I can of your pure grace and glory see.

Help me to value your House more and more

Teach me to walk uprightly and adore

You, Lord of Hosts as I go on my way

Trusting you to guide and keep me day by day.

Chapter 7

Our Furious opponent

Please read Psalm 93

Christian has left the Beautiful House, where he has been taught and refreshed at this house of the Lord. At the house of God, Christian has been warned as he goes on his journey, he will face great difficulties, and so it proves. He descends into the Valley of Humiliation, where he encounters a direct assault from Apollyon, the captain of the devil's guard. This shows one facet of the devil, as we have noted before, that he is a raging foe, a roaring lion seeking whom he may devour. Let us not forget that in the midst of our often very sanitised and mundane lives there is a spiritual maniac; a being who rages and roars in hatred, in implacable enmity against the Christian. That rage is magnified as the Day of Judgement grows nearer and he sees his time of relative freedom get shorter. But it is also magnified by his gnawing frustration that he may fight and hate and rage and attack, but he cannot ever pluck one single Christian from the hand of the Father God. Nonetheless the fury is real, the hatred is implacable and the battle is fierce and we as Christians must put our spiritual armour on and keep it on, if we are to struggle and prevail. This brings us on our journey to **Psalm 93**. The psalmist here is faced with great trials. His response is to turn to the Lord and cry out for help. This psalm shows us how we too can cry for help from God.

The Lord reigns

The first thing the psalmist does is to remind himself of some truths about God, and that these truths do not change. He declares *The Lord reigns.* The word "reigns" means to ascend the throne. Picture this; a certain land is in turmoil, everyone is worried, chaos threatens, but suddenly a trumpet blows the fanfare, and the king appears and majestically ascends the throne. And what a king! We've seen him before in Psalm 24 winning the battle; fantastically dressed; Regal; Majestic; Splendid. Yes he is all that and so it is with God, this psalm is giving a spiritual picture that God is dressed with not with mere robes but with majesty and strength.

So what is verse 1 saying? However it looks to you right now in your life, God is on the throne. In other words, God is actively ruling over his creation, over his enemies, over his subjects. God is reigning over your situation. God, the majestic, all-powerful one is <u>in charge</u>.

He always has

Next we read that this has always been so: from of old, from everlasting. Picture yourself for a moment on the beach. You are watching the sea, and you gaze at a huge ship slowly making its way out to sea. It gets further and further away until it gets to the horizon, and then it disappears from sight. There is a vanishing point, a point beyond sight. That is what this phrase from of old means. God has been on this throne from before you could measure time, from before the vanishing point. That is why the throne is immoveable; it was there before anything else was, everything that has been made has been built around it. It is the foundation of creation and so it cannot be moved and neither can the one be who sits on it. The phrase established his throne literally means, he has made it straight, similar to what we looked at in psalm 1. There is order, symmetry and a plan to everything God does.

Notice here that there is a lot of theology packed into these verses: God is eternal, majestic, reigning, omnipotent, creator and sustainer, and these attributes are fully displayed in his creation (cf. Psalm 19 v 1, Romans 1 v 19-20).

Think about that; the power, majesty, wisdom and unfathomable depths of God stand as a colossus before us. He is an altogether dependable person, we might say, as solid as a rock, but in fact more solid than anything we can imagine. And it is so important in trouble to fix your eyes on that fact, because if you can your trouble gets put into the right perspective, but similarly if you cannot fix your eyes on this your trouble can overwhelm you.

Trouble

The psalmist is in trouble, exactly what kind of trouble we do not know, but that only makes the psalm more useful, because it is applicable to us no matter what the trouble is. The trouble is real. The psalmist is scared, perplexed, despairing. You can hear his panic rising. Look at verse 3: *The floods have lifted up O Lord, The floods have lifted up their voice; The floods have lifted up their waves!* It will be useful to look at the words in detail here. Floods mean <u>seas</u> or <u>oceans</u>. The troubles are not small but are vast, deep and wide. The word, *lifted*, means <u>to raise the head,</u> or, to put their face to my face. How intimidating it is when someone who is much bigger than you puts their face right up close to yours to magnify their threat. The word, *voice* means <u>loud noise,</u> describing the fury of lashing waves. The word, *waves* means a <u>dashing of surf</u> we call them breakers, not some calm swell gently drifting your boat to shore, but smashing, destroying, pounding waves, that can snap a ship in two.

Perhaps you have seen these TV programmes where they have captured on film the results of a hurricane stirring up the sea so that it destroys anything on it, or anything in its path. One such programme was about a house on stilts where the occupants could feel the rising of the waves beneath the house, rising and rising, the noise getting louder and louder, the house starting to thud, and vibrate and then shake and tremble until at last moving more and more frenetically, it was smashed in and carried away by the waves. It is a graphic picture of what this psalmist was feeling about his troubles, and the helplessness of his whole situation. Lord, he cries, these problem are getting big; they're getting too big. Lord, I'm drowning help, Lord, *help!* Peter must have felt like that in Matthew 14 v 30, when he eagerly clambered out of his boat to walk towards Jesus on the water. What a thrill; he was experiencing a miracle. It started off so wonderfully, but then suddenly it got serious, then too serious to deal with until he cried out, Lord, save me.

But, at least the psalmist is praying. He is personally addressing, not some abstract deity, but his own Lord, the one he knows and trusts. What does that Lord do? Do the troubles stop at once? Peter's troubles vanished as soon as he cried out and the Lord caught him. But our troubles don't usually go away like that, do they? These problems of the writer here do not just vanish, and this is so important to notice. Being a Christian does not mean we have no trouble in our lives. Beware of any teaching that tells you otherwise – it is not biblical. Neither do those troubles disappear at once.

That was the lesson the psalmist had to learn. Sometimes our troubles are so huge we are taken like our illustration shows us right to the brink of despair. What then?

The Lord is bigger

The psalmist sees the answer and he gives it to us. The troubles are real, they are frightening, they are looking insurmountable, but, he says, God is bigger than my troubles. However big my trouble, God is bigger: *The Lord on high is mightier than many waters....* Here is the key to how a Christian deals with troubles. It is not what he sees with the eyes of his senses that determine how he deals with his troubles; it is what he sees with the eyes of his <u>faith</u>.

With the eyes of our senses we understand that troubles are there. It is not spiritual to pretend they are not there. No, troubles are real and we have to look them squarely in the face. But, those troubles, though real, are not to be feared. That is the hard part. But because we look at them with the eye of faith we know that God is bigger than these problems. He is in charge of them, and through him we can face them. We must keep in mind that God has allowed them, God has a purpose in them, God will bring you through them; God is mightier than many waters. Later on we will look the words of David in Psalm 23 where he is hemmed in by the valley of the shadow of death. He says serenely I will walk through.

As you go through the Christian life troubles may well come: family problems, job uncertainty, sadness, illness or bereavement. Christians have members of their own family hate them because of their love for Christ. Christians are made redundant. Christians are bereaved. Christians have their spouse leave them for someone else. Christians lose their houses. Christians go bankrupt. There are many evils in the world, many troubles, and these things sometimes happen because we have been true to the Lord and others have cynically and maliciously taken advantage of us and tried to grind us into the dirt. How are you going to deal with that? How are going to cope when you are about to despair? The answer is always the same. Apollyon, in the story came to attack Christian, and he had to fight and prevail. It was a real fight too – a fight to the death. Christian was fighting for his spiritual life. Lose that fight and the journey was over. Turn back and Heaven was lost. What is the key to winning the fight? Thwart Apollyon by using the whole armour of God. As you use it effectively he will flee – resist the devil and he will flee from you says James. We must understand where troubles come from, what their purpose is, but also understand that they are temporary, and because they are temporary they are conquered. That is what gets us through the Valley of Humiliation. No matter how big, angry, noisy, violent, black, rough, sapping, or soaking our waves of trouble are; the Lord is bigger and mightier than them all. They serve his purpose. They have an end.

What about now?

But what do we do in the meantime? Do we sit down and mope? Do we go on spiritual strike? Certainly not. That would be to negate our very calling. No, we must work and fight through our troubles and as we do that we are reminded here that we do something very practical. If you are in a boat leaking water what would you very naturally do? You would not sit with your hands under your chin and say I am waiting for God to work. You would work yourself, and you would do the obvious thing. You would bale out the water coming in. As Christians we bale the water of our troubles. How do we do this? Verse 5 reminds us how. We bale out the water with the word of God. *Your testimonies are very sure.* Testimonies are God's word. The word, *sure* here means support, to build up, to foster, to nurture like a nurse or a parent. In other words God's word is there to build us up, to comfort us, to be our bedrock in uncertain times. The word of God is what the psalmist turns to like he has never done before and we must do the same. Psalm 19 has already told us what the word of God can be to the one who spends time with it, diligently studying it. In the story, Apollyon is put to flight with a good stab from Christian's two-edged sword – the word of God.

The second thing the Psalmist does is to turn to the house of God, and think about how important that is. Where else will he find help? He will find it at the house of God. *Holiness adorns your house, O Lord, forever.* The Lord's house is a holy place, a place where we are taught to be holy, and how to be holy. In times of trouble like no other time we are tempted to play truant from the house of God. We must go. It is absolutely vital that in times of trouble we are in God's house, taking all the succour he provides there. Not to do so is to try to bale out trouble with a bucket with a hole in or to try and row to safety with one oar: we get nowhere.

However, there is more here than a simple exhortation to go to the house of God. Spurgeon quotes in his Treasury[42] that we too are the house of God. We must adorn our life with holiness. In other words we must at all costs guard our lives against any unholiness being allowed to seep in. Instead we must strive to adorn our lives with holy living, holy habits and holy practice. We must keep our fellowship with God intact. The point of trouble from the enemy's point of view is to cut you off from God. Don't make his task one bit easier for him. If we allow sin to reign in our hearts, the Lord will not hear us. In times of trouble the enemy of our soul will tempt us to forget God, to relax our spiritual walk, to put other things first. But the psalmist here warns us against that danger and exhorts to keep

---

[42] The Treasury of David, Volume 2, p.141

ourselves holy. Our house, like the greater house the church, and like our eternal house are everlasting. Guarding our life now, benefits us, the local church, the body of Christ at large and leads us on to heaven. We must never lose sight of how important it is.

Finally

Perhaps, however, you have not become a Christian yet. You have turned to these pages and bypassed the others, because you are in trouble or you have trouble of some kind. Is this message of comfort any good for you? Many people call out to God in times of trouble yet they do not know him. Alas calling out now will not avail, **UNLESS** you are calling on him to answer your greatest need. There is a need above all others, and that is for God to forgive your sins. We all have offended God by the way we have lived our lives, because we have not kept his commandments. We have broken his laws, and the soul that sins shall die. Death is not annihilation; it is eternity in Hell. No problem you will ever have to face can compare to the one you will have when you stand before God on the last day unrepentant and unforgiven. Your first need then is to call upon God to have mercy upon you and forgive your sins. The blood of the Lord Jesus Christ shed upon the cross at Calvary is the only thing that cleanses you from all your sin. God has promised that all who turn to him, confessing their sins, and asking him sincerely for mercy and forgiveness will not be turned away. So come to the Saviour now, and obtain that mercy. After that your life is a new life, because you are living it for the One who loved you and gave himself for you. That doesn't mean you will have no trouble, but it does mean you can take it to the Lord in prayer – that Lord who is bigger than all our troubles.

Jesus gave an apt commentary on this Psalm when he said; In the world you will have tribulation; but be of good cheer, I have overcome the world (John 16 v 33). The teaching of this psalm could be summed up like this:

1. God is in charge

   God allows our troubles

   Turn to God in your trouble

2. God has always been in charge

   God limits our troubles

   Turn to God's provision in trouble

3. God will always be in charge

   God is mightier than our troubles

   Turn to God's holy ways in trouble

The Lord ascends upon the throne

A-Robed in majesty

With strength he's gorgeously attired

So humbly bow your knee

Around this throne the world He built

His power won't wither; strength can't wilt.

Yet floods and waves now threaten me

With noise and angry roar

And smashing power – relentless wrath

Will I become no more?

Yet God, in Christ, is mightier still

He'll say to tempest; Peace, be still"

When troubles pour in as ocean tide

Like Apollyon's fierce assault

Give me the strength O Lord I pray

To fight and not default

With sword of Spirit, holy life

Help me to win in times of strife.

Chapter 8

The Unseen Shepherd

Please read Psalm 23

Christian has been through the Valley of Humiliation – a place of fierce battle and toil. No sooner has he gone through that Valley and recovered somewhat from his wounds gotten in there, than he has to face going through another valley; this time it is the Valley of the Shadow of death. In the first valley we see again the full frontal assault of the evil one; but here the danger is unseen. He is tempted as it were from behind, doubts, fears, temptations, thoughts so subtle, yet so blasphemous, that he doesn't even know whether they are his or not, are whispered into his soul. He is so sorely tried that he really doesn't know which way to turn. It is worse than fighting with Apollyon. Does he go on and stumble blindly into the ditch? Does he go back and give up? Does he just sit down and wait for morning, hoping it will all look better then? This man is under a period of the greatest trials, because it looks and feels as if the journey is over – it is going to end because there is no way through this valley. He is about to die by falling or die by the hand of the hideous creatures around him, or die through just giving up. Yet he comes through. What gets him through are two things: firstly, that he reminds himself that the way to the Celestial City lies through this Valley, and therefore it is not an option to just stop; he has to go keep on going if he is to get through it. And so he goes on in the hope that if he keeps going he will get through. Then, as he is thinking this thought he hears the voice of another man saying; *"though I walk through the valley of he shadow of death, I will fear no ill for you are with me."* With that encouragement as confirmation he goes on until he gets through.

This psalm is the most famous of the psalms. It is entitled simply: *A psalm of David.* The little shepherd "from the sheepcote", as the Authorised Version calls David, writes of the greatest Shepherd of all. You have probably heard this psalm read or sung at funerals, but it deserves a far wider reading than this, because it is a psalm for life – for all our life: in trouble and in joy! There is no evidence as to when David wrote this psalm. It does not say it was written at a funeral, for example of Absalom where David was grief-stricken over the loss of his favourite son, nor at the death of his mighty men. Interestingly also there is no language to allude to David being a king: he may have written it before then either as a shepherd, or on one of those occasions when he was on the run, or when he was in difficulty, or even at the end of his life. Neither is it dedicated to anyone i.e. Chief Musician. It is simply a psalm of David. All the instructions in the psalms have a purpose, but so does a lack of instruction: it seems to me that this psalm is given no narrow focus, because its message is sublime, and it is relevant and helpful in all kinds of trial. It is dedicated by its very lack of a specific dedication to every suffering and needy child of God throughout time. It is dedicated to you, Christian brother or sister, to help you through your darkest hour. It has many themes, but perhaps supremely it is a prayer to God to comfort us in our darkest hour. We will consider this psalm verse by verse.

My Good Shepherd

The first thing I would like you to notice is the word my. *The Lord is my shepherd.* Sometimes, and rightly so, we focus on a psalm's description of the Lord, how he is described, what is said about him and so on, but this psalm is an intensely personal psalm. Whatever it is that has happened to David, it has driven him back into the arms of the Lord, and he is reminding himself of how much he needs the Lord, and what the Lord means to him. The psalm is a comfort psalm to David, and in writing it he is asking the Lord to lead him through his difficulties. Without the word **"my"**, this psalm would merely be an exercise in academic teaching. But David is known and owned by God himself. That is a tremendous statement. It tells us where David wants to be, and where he undeniably is – in the flock of God. There is a personal, intimate and unique relationship between God and the believer. In fact we can add to that when we consider the words of the Lord Jesus when he said, *I am the Good Shepherd.* He deliberately uses the words *I am* to show that he was divine. That was the name by which God revealed himself to Moses and the Israelites. It denotes his timelessness, his supreme greatness and eternal power. *Jehovah is my shepherd,* says the psalmist. Jesus is the Good Shepherd of the flock of God, and therefore I can say: he is my good shepherd, the one who will look after me in every way. This shepherd goes further than the best of shepherds – he lays down his life for his sheep. He died for me, and no-one is going to snatch me out of his hand. I ask you again as I have done previously: Do you know the Lord Jesus like this? Is he your personal Lord and Saviour, or someone who you just know something about? Jesus invites you into his flock: his church. He has paid your entrance fee with his own life-blood, and he offers to you forgiveness of all your sins and new and eternal life. But only he can give it to you: *No man comes to the Father but by me,* he says, but - praise God, that is how we do come.

Because the Lord is my shepherd, *I shall not want.* I will always have what I need: spiritually, physically and materially. What a promise, but it needs to be understood correctly. It is not a promise of worldly wealth and status. In fact as Christians we should not be guilty of setting our hearts on these things at all. Of course we have needs and this is a promise that *my God will supply all your needs in...Christ Jesus,* to use the apostle Paul's words.[43] We may well suffer the loss of all things, but we will have what God determines we need. *Give me neither poverty nor riches – feed me with the food allotted to me,* asked Agur.[44] We are all too prone to cast greedy eyes on what our neighbour (even our Christian neighbour) has, but we must be content with what we have been given, because *those who desire to be rich fall into temptation and a snare.*[45] What a wonderful thing to ask the Lord for our daily bread, and to know that it will be given. But how can we know that that – what are the promises of God toward us?

Feeding

To answer that question, let us take a closer look at what David says. The Lord feeds us. *He makes me to lie down in green pastures. Pasture* means habitation. *Green* means sprouting or new grown. *He leads me beside the still waters. Still* means peaceful. The picture that we have here is that of a family home where the family will flock together to eat and drink. We may eat and drink on our own from time to

---

[43] Philippians 4 v 19
[44] Proverbs 30 v 9
[45] I Timothy 6 v 9

time, but it is the normal, and better, thing to eat together as a family. There are also times when we might meet up with others and go out and eat with them. Food and fellowship go together. So it is in spiritual terms also. We eat and drink on our own when we have what we call our quiet time, that time of specially being alone with the Lord. That is good, healthy and right. But we also go to the house of the Lord to eat and drink with the Lord's people. It is there that the Lord in a special way meets with and feeds his people. It is there we receive our much-needed spiritual nourishment. A much-used theme of David in his psalms is the emphasis on going to meet with God's people in the house of the Lord.[46] Christian you must not try to get out of going to church – especially in times of difficulty – but you should be there on every occasion that you can, because it is there that the Lord will meet with you and feed your soul. Would you starve yourself physically? Why is it you so often starve your soul? Faith comes by hearing and hearing by the word of God. The Word of God is our essential spiritual food: without it we are as weaklings starved of our basic nutrition and putty in the hands of our spiritual opponent.

---

[46] See Psalms 5 v 7; 26 v 8; 27 v 4; 36 v 8; 55 v 14; 65 v 4

Restoring

The Lord revives his people. *He restores my soul.* To restore here literally means: to return to the starting point. We need restoring because we are in a fight; because we sin; and because we just get plain weary.

We are in a spiritual war. We have an enemy who is determined to make us ineffective soldiers – soldiers who achieve nothing for the Lord. Satan longs to see us lazy, apathetic, indifferent and worldly. We have to fight against these things for they naturally appeal to old natures. Remember always that you are a pilgrim on a one-way journey and our enemy is determined to deflect us into the ditch (the "quagmire" Bunyan graphically calls it), stop us still in our tracks or best of all turn us back. We need to fight just to keep going. The Lord encourages us along the way. He does this in his word, and by the fellowship we have with him and our fellow believers. In Bunyan's story the Pilgrim, Christian, heard those great words of encouragement from another pilgrim, and it spurred him on greatly.

This meaning of returning us to the starting point is vital when we fall into sin. When we sin, we are alienated again from God: our fellowship is interrupted. Sometimes that sin is deliberately done. What happens then? If we sin we break our fellowship with God. We must go straight back and confess our sins, and be forgiven and cleansed all over again – we must return to the starting point.

Sometimes, to use Paul's words, we just become weary in well doing. We have been zealous for the Lord and we are worn out. We need to come apart and rest awhile. Wherever, when ever and however we do this will depend upon our circumstances, but when we do we must take time to think about what we are doing, evaluate it before the Lord, and just ask ourselves the questions: Am I doing what God wants me to be doing; how do I know; is the Lord blessing this work: and again ask how do I know? You see we can be busy, busy, busy but not be using our time and gifts wisely. We need to ask, ourselves if we are being busy – yet so busy we have lost sight of what we are doing. Satan can use our "busyness" to render us useless, we're so stretched we have no strength to do anything well. It is a good thing to take it all to the Lord in prayer at regular times and just check that we really are in the place where he wants us to be. Do so carefully, and do so remembering the Lord's concern for you. *Come to me,* said the Lord Jesus, *and I will give you rest.*[47] In times of busyness and hard work, and with that, often, discouragement, return regularly to the starting point and let the Lord revive your soul.

---

[47] Matthew 11 v 29-30

What is the result of such refreshment? *He leads me in the paths of righteousness for his name's sake.* The Lord will show us the right way to go. He does this for our benefit and to bring honour to his name. This is a great comfort when we seek the Lord's leading. There are often times when we do not know what to do next. At that time remember what the Lord has said. *I will instruct you and teach you in the way you should go. I will guide you with my eye.*[48] There is often a dilemma about guidance in the Christian life, and this is not the place to give a great treatise on it. Suffice to say that very much more than we often do, we must take the Lord at his word – literally. Couple this trust with an honest desire to actually <u>do</u> God's will, and we cannot go far wrong. It is here in black and white.

Battling

So now we have been refreshed, fed and instructed by the Lord: what comes next? It is back to the battle. We have mentioned this, but we need to add to it a little more. We have a grim opponent whose aim is to render us null and void. We have to fight. David pictures it like this; *Yea, though I walk through the valley of the shadow of death...*

---

[48] Psalm 32 v 8

Sometimes the Christian life is so hard it seems unbearable. Bunyan pictured it like this:

> ...as far as this valley reached... on the right hand there was ditch...on the left a quag... The pathway is narrow... and so dark he knew not where to set it next... Flame and smoke would come in abundance, with sparks and hideous noises... Thus he went on a great while; he heard great noises, as it were, rushing towards him so that he thought he would be torn in pieces.... He heard a company of fiends coming forward to meet him, he stopped, half thought whether to go back... he resolved to go on...then one of the wicked ones got behind him...softly...and whisperingly suggested many blasphemies to him which he thought proceeded from his own mind...this put Christian to it more than anything that he met with before to think he should now blaspheme him that he loved so much before, yet if he could have helped it he would not have done it...[49]

I have quoted a large piece here, because as a whole extract it really gives us a picture of how awful and terrifying it is to go through this valley of the shadow of death. Perhaps death has touched your life and its shadow is cast over your whole existence. Nothing escapes it; you cannot go outside it into the sunshine of happiness even for a minute. You wonder if you will ever escape it again. At that

---

[49] Pilgrims Progress, p77

time you may wonder if you even or ever had a Christian life. Where is your hope now?

Perhaps other traumas have hit you. We as Christians are not spared the troubles of the world, sometimes in fact we have more, for we can be persecuted or targeted in some way because of our faith. How do we survive? David knew all about these things, and there are no trite answers to our pain, whether it be physical, spiritual or mental. They all happen to us, and they are all real – denial is not an option for us. Instead we have to find an answer. What is it? Notice in this verse that David states facts not feelings. He does not rely on how he feels. That is a most powerful, yet most unreliable emotion. Instead he relies on what he cannot see, and that is the hand of the Lord in it all. He says: *I will walk through.* This is so positive. *I will,* tells me that this walking through is definite: it is going to happen – fact. *Walk,* tells me how I will get through this: not on my belly, crawling, but walking: purposeful, upright, with direction, measured, progressive. Yet it is walking, not running, for there are no quick fixes to this kind of pain. Sorrow and anguish do not disappear overnight. They do diminish (even if we feel they never will), slowly, but they do diminish at a steady measured pace where each day brings us through another small piece of progress. At the end of that day we may not feel any further forward at all, but we are one day nearer being out of that valley. Put those days together and surely the valley end comes nearer and near

until there is glimpse of sun, then a bit more and there does

come a time when we are *through*. I will walk through, says

David. Tell yourself that every day – however many days

there are - until you are.

But one thing we often wonder is why we are going

through these things in the first place. I cannot tell you

specifically of course, but it is certainly true that Satan

wants us off the path – retiring from the battle, and into

the ditch. He wants us to give up, to believe we are so bad,

so useless, so timid there is no point going on. That is why in

the story these creatures are depicted as going up to

Christian and whispering these things to him and why he is

almost convinced at first that he can never get through.

Note what the Lord provides us with: *Your rod and staff*

they comfort me. What would you comfort a sorrowing

person with? The Lord provides a rod and a staff. The rod is

a rod correction and the staff denotes a walking stick of

help. This shows us the Lord's concern in our sorrow, but he

doesn't take it magically away. This tells us that he is

allowing it and he has a supreme purpose in it. Nothing is

random, or fateful or chancy. Knowing that the Lord wants

to correct us and strengthen us on our journey may sound

harsh, especially if as far as we can tell we have not sinned.

But notice the word *comfort* here. It is not a word, which

means casual sympathy, as we often give one another, but

rather it means deep empathy. Weep with those who weep we are told[50], The Lord having endured every kind of trial we can ever endure, knows how to weep with us, when we bitterly shed tears in our times of sorrow. He loves us with an everlasting love. When we go through troubles so hard it is like walking through where the sun does not shine and the light at the end cannot be seen, the Lord is walking it with us. He says: *Be strong and of good courage...be not afraid, nor dismayed... I will never leave you nor forsake you... I will be with you wherever you go.*[51] It does not lessen what has happened to us, neither does it stop it hurting, but it does reassure us that we will walk through these troubles and get to the other side.

Blessing

Look at the words used here in verse 5. Spurgeon puts it like this: The warrior feasted, the priest anointed, the guest satisfied.[52] Although there are hard times in our Christian life, it is not a life of drudge and drear. It is a life of fellowship with the Lord. In the midst of all the enemies spiritual and literal that we have, the walk of the Christian is filled with good things. We are warriors. The Lord has set a table of provision for us. No soldier fights on an empty

---

[50] Romans 12 v 15
[51] Joshua 1 vv 6-9
[52] Treasury of David, Volume I p.373

stomach, and neither can we. The Lord feeds us. We are priests: those set aside to serve God night and day. All priests have to be consecrated with holy oil and appointed to their place. The Holy Spirit anoints us and appoints us to be servants of the Most High God, and it is our privilege to serve him wherever he has put us. We are also guests, for the Lord has invited us to come. He has chosen us, bought us and saved us. But he does not stop there. He gives and gives and gives again until our *cup runs over.* God is not mean with his blessings to us, but generous. Every day there is more than enough grace and help to take us through whatever it is our lot to accomplish.

David adds that our enemies are powerless to stop God blessing us right under their noses. This reminds us that Satan, though powerful, is limited. Although he schemes against us constantly, he cannot prevent the Lord's provision for us, nor thwart the Lord's purposes for us. What we must be careful to avoid is doing his work for him, by absenting ourselves from the Lord's provision – his house, his word and his people.

Heaven

Surely goodness and mercy shall follow me all the days of my life. Surely means definitely, certainly. The language of the psalm reminds us again that we are on a journey a journey through life and to the City of the Lord – as the hymn-writer puts it; a march to Zion, and will get there. Nothing can stop that, no matter how fierce the battle. Heaven is ours. God grants me these wonderful blessings each day – his *goodness and mercy,* but one day I will not need them, for the battle will be over, and hope will be replaced by sight. The daily provision of faith shall not be necessary, and neither will the need for mercy to forgive my sin for I shall sin no more. David is there already in the *house of the Lord – forever.* And, *I shall dwell* there too. To dwell means to reside as a permanent resident – Home! The Lord is now preparing a place for us to live with him – in paradise.

We see here in this psalm that the battle in part is what we can see versus what we cannot see. In times of trial (part of the trial actually) we feel all is lost – we will never get through this. Bunyan in the House of the Interpreter has Christian watch a fire burning and Satan throwing water on it – yet the fire doesn't go out. In fact, it gets hotter and brighter. Why, he asks? He is taken around the back – behind the scenes as it were, and he sees the Lord pouring oil on the flames, keeping them burning. Feelings of sorrow, loss, hurt, anger, unfairness, despair threaten to overwhelm us, but behind all that the Lord our Good Shepherd is still feeding us, comforting us guiding us and walking with us. And you will get through…that's a promise.

As I go on my pilgrimage
The Shepherd leads the way
He makes me lie by pastures green
And feasts me every day

My weary soul he does revive
In righteous paths I walk
For the sake of his dear name
To trust in him I'm taught

I have to walk in blackest shade
Of death's deep vale of tears
But your rod and staff of comfort
Preserve my soul from fears

I will walk through - O blessed hope
To the table spread for me
And though my enemies gnash in vain
My blessing they shall see

So, all through life my Saviour leads
With mercy and with good
I will in the Lord's house dwell
And taste Eternal food

Chapter 9

Vanity Fair

Please read Psalm 37 (and also Psalms 56 & 119)

In the story of Pilgrim's Progress we read that having come through the Valley of the Shadow of Death, Christian is joined on his pilgrimage by Faithful. A companion on the way is so helpful. Sometimes we have these people who come into our lives who are a real boon to us on our way. They are "a companion of the one who fears you; and of those who keep your precepts" 119:63.They may be family, lifelong friends or a spouse. They may be people who have come into our lives for a short time. But, they are sent by the Lord, who orders all things for our good, to do us good. Psalm 119:68 says of the Lord: "you are good and you do good".

Christian and Faithful now come in our story to the place which is the very epitome of the world's opposition to God and his people: to Vanity Fair. Here was openly and brazenly the opportunity to indulge in any and every worldly desire – whether it were good and lawful or wicked and despicable. The point of the Fair we are told was that it was deliberately set up by Beelzebub, Apollyon and Legion to make the pilgrims stop their journey and settle in the town of Vanity. Here and now Christian has to stop and decide what is going to take priority in his life. Will he settle in Vanity Fair and enjoy the things it offers or continue on his pilgrimage? This question is one of the hardest for the pilgrim. It would be so easy to justify spending just a little time indulging himself in a little pleasure after all he has been through. But, heeding Evangelist's warning of the danger, Christian and Faithful show no interest in stopping their pilgrimage and dallying in the delights of the Fair, and so they quickly became the objects of derision and defamation. Christian and Faithful are arrested, falsely accused, beaten and imprisoned. Christian escapes with his life, but Faithful is martyred. It is a fact that when we don't join in with the pleasures of this world, we incur the wrath of the world. It is like a spoilt child which demands we play with their toys, to their rules, at its whim.

When we consider the subject of how the world treats the Christian pilgrim, the questions are often difficult and painful. David himself exclaims: "When will you execute judgment on them that persecute me" (119:84)? There is an impatient, frustrated tone in that cry. Why does God allow these things? How do they get away with it? Why does God not strike the wicked down where he stands? And... how do we cope with both the evil itself and the sense of injustice we feel? A general answer is this: In a war there are always casualties. The difference in this war is that – as Faithful found – the pilgrim's death grants him a crown of life and an immediate escort into the courts of Heaven.

But before we go on to consider this psalm we need to stop and bring something to mind. Have you ever asked why does Satan attack the Christian at all? We are told that the three pronged attack is the world, the flesh and the devil. Why does he bother? After all, we are saved and secure; nothing can alter that. The devil is no fool and he knows the truth of that perfectly well. In chapter 7 we find the devil in the form of a ferocious enemy attacking Christian full on. Here in this chapter we find him setting up the town of Vanity Fair with the express aim of using the enticements of the world from stopping the Christian going any further on his journey: First the lion, then the snake (I Peter 5:8; II Corinthians 11:3). Why – if he knows he cannot win, *why* bother trying? What is the root and basis of the devil's opposition to the Christian pilgrim?

Looking at it from the devil's point of view we can see the answers. When Adam sinned, all mankind fell into the kingdom of darkness. Satan, having won the battle in the Garden of Eden (and in spite of the promise God made to Adam in his hearing) regards all mankind as his property: as his subjects, because they have become separated from God through sin and are God's enemies. Therefore when a man or woman becomes a Christian, for the devil it is unexpected – as he does not know who the elect are in advance – and an act of treason. As in any walk of life traitors are despised, so will the implacable enemy of God despise the one who deserts his camp, his cause and his kingdom for the enemy – for God. For all Satan's power, cunning and might, and for all the guile and strategies he has at his disposal, he has a dwindling kingdom: every day the devil sees people leaving it, and his rage and sense of impotence increases with every deserter. Therefore the devil hates the Christian with unquenchable malice, and though he has lost him, will never, ever allow him any peace for a moment. But he has another pressing problem to deal with and that is what further damage to his kingdom the traitor might do. He therefore needs to negate his witness as much as possible so that the one who has deserted him doesn't aid and abet others deserting him also. So, for the devil it is a twin strategy of vengeance and damage limitation. On one hand with unremitting wrath he aims to inflict as much misery as possible on the Christian pilgrim, but more importantly and shrewdly is the second aim; to render the Christian as useless a soldier, an ambassador and a witness to the truth of God as possible, so that no more traitors desert his cause. Writers of old would say that there are three strands of temptation used against the Christian: the world the flesh and the devil. In Chapter 7 we see Satan use direct opposition to stop (or drown) the pilgrim; "the Devil". In the next chapter we see how he uses the "the Flesh". Here we see him use the third strategy "the World".

So when we look at Psalm 37 we see some specific answers to the questions above. Matthew Henry called this psalm: "An exposition in some of the hardest chapters in the book of Providence"[53] How does David, who wrote this Psalm, deal with these issues? What experience had he had of the enemy's schemes? In answer it must be said that David had a wealth of experience of the devil's wrath to draw upon. He had been hounded almost to death by his own father-in-law, King Saul. His friend Ahimelech the priest was killed in cold blood by Saul's henchman Doeg because he had given David food, thinking he was on official business. His great friend and brother-in-law Jonathan was tragically killed in battle. He had had his wise friend Ahithophel desert him. His own son Absalom tried to usurp his throne and have him killed. Another son, Amnon, had forced his sister Tamar, and then had been murdered by Absalom. David knew all about the devil's schemes and also about wicked men and what they could do. Here is how he answers the questions above.

Keep your head and keep your perspective

---

[53] P613

The striking thing about this psalm is that it is a psalm of great certainty and assurance. It says very definitely: "Do not fret; do not be envious; cease from anger; forsake wrath and cease from evil". These verbs are imperatives: to fret literally means to blaze up; we would say to flare up. The verb "anger" gives a picture of a huge beast snorting as he prepares to trample his tormentor. The word "wrath" is even stronger: it carries the meaning, to poison from its fever. When you are in pain or distress your body releases toxins which poison your system if there are too many of them, and you quickly become ill. To give place to the wrath we may feel at times is to poison your own soul just as toxins will poison your body. So, the psalmist concludes in verse 8 do not fret – it only causes harm.

Now we must ask: How can you say this? What is the basis for these instructions – especially in the face of people doing me such wrong? The answer is this: There is a certainty which lies behind this psalm which is not taught assertively, but assumptively, and that is, *a great Assize is going to take place* (37:13). If you read all through the psalm its whole context and basis is, of this judgment, and the certainty that the "Judge of all the earth will do right". There will be a day when the Judge of all the earth will judge all men who have lived throughout time and throughout the world. No one will escape – all will receive the summons and the escort to take them before the Judge. Therefore the lesson is: look at the big picture and remember nothing in this life is forever no matter how grim it is. Do not take matters into your own hands; repay no man evil for evil, because each crime, each transgression, each hurt has been reported and the trial date already written down. There is a judgment to face. All who commit sin will answer for it, but those who specifically hurt God's children will be in the gravest of dangers. It is very easy for us to forget how much God loves us isn't it? God sent his Son to die for us. He did that because he loves us with an everlasting love. That love will never change, fade or falter. When we are persecuted for our faith look at the promises we invoke: "Put my tears in your bottle... in your book. Every insult, every hurt we receive for being a Christian is recorded in God's book. Every tear we shed is, as it were, tenderly put in God's bottle for Him to look at with sorrow and remind Him of our pain. How will our tormentors feel when they see those things in God's hands? "He that touches you", declares Zechariah, the prophet, "touches the apple of his eye". Moses in his last words to God's people told them, that "The eternal God is your refuge and underneath are the everlasting arms..." the Lord Jesus solemnly declared: "Better if a millstone be hung around his neck and be cast into the depths of the sea", than to meet the angry God and Father of the children you have hurt. God loves his people, more protectively than any Mum, more dotingly than any Dad we can think of. Woe to those who arrogantly and foolishly think they can hurt us and escape the wrath of the Most High God. So, in the heat of the battle and the anguish of the hurt, we must remember these things, keep our heads, and keep our perspective.

Keep doing the right things

With that great comfort in mind, how do we get on with our lives? What do we actually do instead? There are a lot of very strongly worded imperatives we must take note of. Look at verses 3, 4, 5, 7 and we read we must "Trust; Dwell; Feed; Delight; Commit; Rest". And we have all these commands in the face of great trial, hurt and confusion. E. M. Blaiklock wrote: It is a hard world: It censures grief as lack of faith...it taunts misfortune as proof of atheism.[54] Psalm 42 concurs with this when the psalmist laments those who taunt him "Where is your God". Is there a God – if there is at all, you are foolish to believe in and trust him. But David writes the opposite. When we are tempted to despair, to retaliate, to get angry with God or man or perhaps the hardest of all when we are trying to understand what has happened and why it has happened, in that moment we must obey these commands. Rather than fret with our circumstances we trust, rest and so on. these words are very

---

[54] Commentary on the Psalms Volume 1: Page 105

encouraging and they are very strong in the original and full of meaning: Trust is to go to a place of refuge; Feed is to graze; tend a flock with pasture, but figuratively to associate with one as a friend; delight is to be soft or luxurious – we might say exquisite – there is a thought of revelling in the enjoyment of God in that word. Rest is only used in this way once in the Old Testament and means "to be dumb"; to just stop. Plumer says that it means, like Aaron in Leviticus 3:3, to acquiesce[55]. Wait (in verse 7) means to stay oneself[56]. Again we have this picture of self-control. To cease means; to trample oneself or, to prostrate, as before a king. You get the picture by now I'm sure. Roll all these imperative commands together and you have a picture of a military commander telling his troops to halt, to unpack their kit and to take a breather. Enjoy the view, take in the air and sit back and watch the champion take the fight to the enemy. This is not weakness, but strength. This is not giving up, but going on. Keep doing the right things. "The bumps", says the title of a book, "are what you climb on". So, when you are laughed at, remember so was the Lord, when you are beaten, lied to, lied about, defamed, rejected, stolen from, hurt in any way for the Lord's sake or because you are the Lord's, or yet because, like Job, the devil wants to try your faith out to see what it's made of, then you must respond in

---

[55] p450
[56] According to Young.

obedience to these commands: trust; rest; delight; commit; wait; and feed. In doing so, you will do good to yourself and heap coals on the heads of those who hate you and despitefully use you.

Keep remembering what you have now is better

This psalm doesn't just focus on the outright opposition to the world: there is another strategy. Satan wants us to drop what we have now, like an old toy, and look over at what the world has. What others have always seems much better than what we have doesn't it? It isn't, because God has allotted our portion and what we have is the best for us. It comes out of the storehouse of God's providence and we should never scorn or despise the good gifts of our Heavenly Father. The presents we have may be strange to us yet they are his choice. In the film *"Paycheck"*, Ben Affleck's character is given an incomprehensible set of worthless looking items instead of the millions of dollars he expects. But as the film unravels so does the meaning and the value of the useless looking items, until in the end he gains the treasure that is rightfully his by promise. It is the same for us. God may give us things, and take us places we find ordinary and useless and with no value, but they are the tools with which must accomplish our mission for him. What is the mission: to glorify him in everything say, do and are.

And so the second part of the psalm is focused also on the provision of God to his people.

Now, in case you accuse me of being too heavenly minded to be of any earthly use, let's get practical. The future is secured, but what about the present? We've said that right now what we have is better than the wicked man's portion v 16, no matter how much he has. It is too stereotypical to assume the godly man is poor and the wicked are rich, but it is often a fact of life, because of the obsession many have with money. They understand the things that money brings: status, goods and power. But whatever the ungodly have, it is not as good as the poorest man of God, neither will it do him or her any good in the life to come. But having said that what do God's people have NOW?

- Firstly they have an assurance of God's presence with them every step of the way v23. There is an unseen but ever faithful co-pilgrim with the pilgrim: every step, every day. You may heard the phrase: "You'd want him with you in the trenches" My brother is 6 feet plus, big, strong and well-muscled. If I were to go to somewhere scary he'd be the man I'd want beside me! You see the point? The Lord is with us always. What a wonderful, comforting thought.

- Next we have the promise that though we fall, the Lord will hold on to us and pick us up again. Think of the determined toddler who is beginning to walk. He sees something he wants and strives to get it. He falls, the parent picks him up, he falls again and the parent is there again. And so it goes on until he reaches where he wants to go. The parent is always there, and there patience never runs out. How much more with God? The pilgrim can truthfully say: He will pick me up when I fall, and comfort me and set me on my way again.

- Thirdly God's people are indestructible until their pilgrimage is over. Nothing can thwart God's steps that he has planned for them v28. They will go where he sends them, achieve what he has marked out for them and complete the mission he has sent him or her upon. There is therefore a point to the pilgrimage, a purpose and a plan. That is a wonderful thing because surely there can nothing more futile than a life lived just aimlessly wandering around tasting this and trying that but all to no purpose. The pilgrim has a chosen path, a chosen way and a chosen destiny.

- Fourthly they are provided for v 25. Even though the pilgrim may be poor and despised by the rest of the people they mix with, the Lord will provide for them.

This psalmist gives his testimony and it is to God's provision for his people. Whilst God's people are to work diligently and be hardworking and faithful in all they do, they are not to fret over how they will eat or what they will wear because the Lord knows they have need of these things and will always provide. The experience and life stories of older people are fascinating aren't they? I enjoy listening to tales of old men and women telling me their life stories, whether it was in the war or in their job or with their adventures in life – what they did where they went, what they saw and so on. Their testimony is thrilling and often so unexpected. Here is the psalmist's testimony: it is that though he is now old, he has always seen God provide for each one of his people.

Keep the end in sight

The pilgrimage is a journey. Some journeys, like Chairman Mao spoke of, are a thousand miles and must start with one small step. But all journeys end. After verse 8 this psalm is focused firmly on the end of the journey. How will things be when my journey ends, we may ask? Notice the use of this word "shall". It appears 28 times after verse 8. There are promises for God's people and curses against those who persecute them. Evildoers will be cut off, they shall wither, they shall be no more; they will perish, whose day is coming, whose sword shall enter their own heart, whose arms will be broken. These are terrible things to speak of, and perhaps do not sit comfortably with our way of looking at those who hurt us. And of course we must not be those who rail and curse and wish these things on any one. They are not so much deprecatory as solemn statements of fact. They are not things we wish on anyone, but they are the doom of the unrepentant. The Christian pilgrim on the other hand looks forward to a great inheritance (vv 9, 11, 18, 22, 29, 34), to peace, and everlasting life. These are great and precious promises. We are bound up with what we have here, with what we can see with our eyes and feel with our senses, but laid up for God's people is this wonderful paradise where God will always be with his people and where there will be peace, and love and safety and a total absence of evil and wickedness of any kind. The psalmist talks in very definite terms. There is no room for any misunderstanding here.

R. L. Stevenson wrote: "to travel hopefully is better than to arrive", and the early Taoists adage was "The journey is the reward". That may be true of a steam train ride, but for the Christian pilgrim it isn't. Keep the destination in mind. Keep the end in sight.

Do not fret when evil strikes

Satan cannot do just what he likes

Although his staff work evil yet

They'll be cut down so do not fret

Trust in the Lord do good and rest.

Feed on him, recline – be blessed

Commit to Him tho' the way be yet

Hard and bleak – just do not fret

The wicked plots against the just

Satan can't win, but try he must

His sword of enmity he'll whet

The Lord just laughs, so do not fret.

I was young and now am old

I have seen – if truth be told -

The righteous fed, his needs all met

So give, and lend, and do not fret

Though wicked men are in great power

The day will come when they'll be no more

The Lord will save – He's paid your debt

So eternity beckons – do not fret

Chapter 10

Off the beaten track

Please read Psalm 51

We have followed Pilgrim through his recent trials. They have been terrible to bear, and yet the Lord has taken him though them. Life now is good. He has got a new travelling companion; he has had a time of refreshing and rest. It is just at such a time that he needed to be on his guard, but he goes astray. He also takes his companion astray with him. It started off as a small thing; they took a decision to do something they really knew they shouldn't. Then as they became aware that something was amiss, they tried to undo what they had done and go back. They found that they could not. Their dilemma grew worse and worse until they were stumbling along blindly not knowing where they were going or what they were doing. Then they were caught, imprisoned and beaten until their spirits were crushed. They were prisoners of Giant Despair, and locked in Doubting Castle.

Perhaps you are a Christian: saved: redeemed: A new person walking in the ways of God. Perhaps you have been a little careless in your own Christian walk. On a certain day you wake up like any other but on this day you sin. You sin greatly against the Lord. Perhaps you think you never have or ever will do such a thing. I guess that David thought the same. He would have wept bitter tears if he could have seen into the future. What went so, so wrong? What happened that David should do this? It started off as a small thing; he got careless. He was in the wrong place at the wrong time. He should have been fighting his battles, but he stayed at home in idleness. He then was tempted. He sinned. He panicked, and he tried to cover up what he had done, but made it worse by committing more sins. We read these terrible words; what David had done *displeased the Lord* (II Samuel 11 v 27). Is that where you are at this moment? Have you done something wrong of which you are ashamed? Do you feel that you can never come back to the Lord? Do you hear in your spiritual ears the enemy of souls whispering to you that you have reneged on your profession and the Lord doesn't want you any more? Do not despair. God has not, will not ever cast you off. But you do need to deal with what has happened. David hardened his heart for the best part of a year. On the outside everything looked the same. He got on with his life. His servants who knew what had gone on kept quiet, yet they must have been appalled at David's actions. Perhaps they whispered about it whilst David was not around. But David was oblivious. He thought the whole nasty business had gone away. Then there came a day when Nathan the prophet came to him – courageously – and shattered his pompous self-justification. David was humbled, and then he wrote this most famous of psalms. It is his psalm of repentance. In it he seeks the Lord's forgiveness for these sins of the wickedest kind. This psalm may surprise you. It might also shock you. In a way I hope it does, because it may mean that I have shown you afresh the amazing ness of the grace of God in the gospel. What David had lost was his relationship with God. This to him was worse than any punishment he would have to bear for his sin. He would suffer terribly for what he had done, and he knew it, but all that mattered right now was to get back into fellowship with God.

Spiritually stained

The first thing that David deals with is the sin itself. It is hard to believe these verses are Old Testament verses for he does not appeal to the Levitical sacrificial system. Notice that he does not bring an offering to God. He instead goes direct to God in prayer and he says; *Have mercy on me O God, according to your lovingkindness; according to the multitude of your tender mercies, blot out my transgressions.* What is he doing? He is on his knees and he pleads for mercy. He offers no excuse, nor any mitigating circumstances. Mercy! Mercy! Mercy! David goes to God in abject repentance and sorrow and contrition. He begs that

God will not treat him as he deserves, but that he will have mercy.

You know, all our sin needs to be dealt with in the same way: the little and the big. Sin is a stench in God's nostrils. He hates it unquenchably. All too often you and I are prone to seek excuses for our sins, but God will have none of it. David so to speak holds his hands up and in effect says there is no excuse for what I have done, and that is what we must do too.

Spiritually smelly

Wash me thoroughly from my iniquity, and cleanse me from my sin. David recognises that he stinks to high heaven. He cannot get rid of the stain and smell of it himself. Well did Shakespeare understand this as he depicts Lady Macbeth forlornly washing her hands trying to get rid of the guilt she bears, saying mournfully: *Here's the smell of blood still: all the perfumes of Arabia will not sweeten this little hand.* Sin is like an obstinate smell that will not go away. It clings to you stubbornly and will not let you go. David had committed the foulest of sins. He had coveted another man's wife. He had committed adultery. He had been deceitful. He had been treacherous to a man loyal to him, one who was not even an Israelite but was nonetheless prepared to fight and die for him. David was to write: *Even my own familiar friend in whom I trusted, who ate my bread, has lifted up his heel against me* (Psalm 41 v 9). David had done exactly the same to Uriah. He orchestrated his death. David in effect murdered his own soldier. Just how much did his sin stink to high heaven? God alone knew.

An honest assessment

For I acknowledge my transgression and my sin is ever before me: Look again at David's choice of words. He knew what he had done: *iniquity* (v2) means to be perverse, to go crooked; *transgression* means to revolt. David is giving an honest assessment of how things really are. Now that he has his spiritual senses back he realises he is spiritually empty. This emptiness has lasted a long time. It has been a year before David has come to his senses, for it wasn't until Nathan came after Bathsheba gives birth that David prays. During that time David's fellowship with God had slipped away and gone. But David had not realised it. No doubt he went to the tabernacle as he always did. No doubt he prayed. No doubt he talked a good spiritual talk, but his spiritual walk had stopped. He wasn't marching to Zion. He was, in every way, staying at home. When we sin and do not deal with it straightaway something happens. We ignore the Spirit's prompting our conscience and we harden our heart. The longer this goes on the harder our hearts become, because each day we are reinforcing that decision. It is like putting layer upon layer on a concrete path; until it is so strong and so hard it seems unbreakable. We have become almost like we were before we were saved. The form of spiritual life might be there, but its vibrancy – its very life – is ebbed away like the neap tide. David knew this. He also knew that there was one remedy, and that was to own up completely. *I acknowledge my sins,* he said. I declare them. Here they are Lord. Please deal with them for me.

A spiritual judgement

Against you, you only have I sinned... David passes sentence on himself. Once when playing in a football match, I handled the ball on the goal-line. As soon as I realised what I had done, I walked off the pitch, because there was only one outcome of my transgression – the red card! There could only be one judgement: one sentence, one punishment. When we break God's law there is only one person whom we sin against – God! Now you might find this disturbing. What about Uriah? What terrible things happened to this blameless and honest man! Surely he had been sinned against? No, Uriah had been terribly wronged and for that wrong David (and his household) were terribly punished[57], but it was against God – the supreme lawgiver - and him alone that sin had been committed. David knew it was God he had to answer to. It was God who had set him up on the throne of Israel, preserved him in all his battles, given him

---

[57] See II Samuel 12 vv 7 -18

everything that heart could wish for, but David had thrown it all back in God's face and stolen something that wasn't his. God's laws had been broken and David faces the facts. We must do the same or else we cannot even begin to have our sins dealt with. God requires first of all our honest grasp of the situation.

Sin needs purging

Purge me with hyssop... The thing to realise as we read this psalm together is that David understands exactly what has got to happen if he is to be forgiven. The Old Testament sacrifices simply will not do. He uses this word purge. This word purge here is means *expiate* or *bear the blame*. David had an amazing grasp on what needed doing. David knew his sin had to be blotted out, not swept under the carpet. Who could do this? He couldn't. He has the faith to actually ask God to do it for him. *Will you,* he asks, *bear my sin away for me.* As we watch this request go to heaven, to our amazement God agrees and hold's David's sin in account, as it were, until Jesus came and literally did bear away his sin, and the sin of countless others, to the cross and nailed them there. That is the gospel. That is what as Christians we have all grasped onto and been saved by. Why then does it surprise us? Because when we see a real situation like this it brings it home to us just what God has done.

The crux of the matter

How is it that God can forgive David? How is it we never read of David going to God through the Levitical system of offerings? How could God forgive this man's terrible sins? Here we come to the crux of the matter: *For you do not desire sacrifice or else I would give it. The sacrifices of God are a broken spirit, a broken and contrite heart - These O God you will not despise.* David knew the mechanical act of killing animals would not change his relationship with God one tiny little bit. God wasn't looking for dead meat. Asaph knew that also; see Psalm 50 v 12-14 and Isaiah 1 vv 11-15. God wanted living repentance, and that is what David offered. That is why he was forgiven. David brought his broken heart to God, not his excuses or his rituals, or even his mitigating circumstances. He came broken up inside at what he had done, and he begged for mercy. What he had done in sinning like this was to snatch back control of his life from the Lord whom he had given it to all those years ago. That is what we do when we sin. Now he hands it back, broken and tattered – what a mess he'd made of it - and he asks God to mend it and own it again.

Does it seem like David got away with it a bit lightly? A catalogue of evil like this, and then a prayer and all is forgiven and forgotten? Not really: in fact, not at all. You see in this prayer David is not just saying a form of words or muttering a formula. He is giving his life back to God. That decision will cost him everything he is and has. When we repented of our sin the first time we gave up our lives to God. We became Christians, disciples of the Lord Jesus, and we did not from that moment own ourselves any more. We are his servants. Furthermore we are living sacrifices – our whole lives are from now on not to be used to please ourselves, but the one who loved us and gave himself for us. Repentance is indeed free. The consequences of repentances are absolute. David in his act of repentance is saying all this to God. When we fall into sin, no matter how catastrophic that sin is we must do exactly the same as David, and mean it as he did.

The bigger picture

Do good in your good pleasure to Zion; Build the walls of Jerusalem. Then you shall be pleased with the sacrifices of righteousness, with burnt offerings and whole burnt offering; then they shall offer bulls on your altar. At the end of a film, which has been solely involved with the plight of a main character, the director has the camera zoom out. The camera goes wider and wider whilst the character becomes smaller and smaller until he or she is a dot on a very big landscape. This is to show the viewer that there is a bigger picture, a broader canvass and the character whose life has been the sole object in the film is as it were placed back into his right (and small) place and perspective in society. David does the same. He ends the psalm by talking about the bigger picture – the people of God as a whole.

David recognised that his sin has had consequences for himself and for others. When the king went astray from God, God's promise of protection was forfeit. Being forgiven would not change this. God's name was blasphemed among the nations because of David's sin. Uriah's family were bereaved because of David's sin. Bathsheba had to marry David and instead of being the sole love of one man, was part of a horde of David's women competing even to be noticed, let alone loved. God's people suffered because of David's sin. There would be rebellion, civil war, humiliation and bloodshed because of David's sin. David recognised all this, and he prays for the people that God would bless them, as well as himself. In sinning David had allowed spiritually at least the walls of Zion to be broken down, the enemy of souls to come swaggering in and spoil the spiritual well-being of God's people. Now they needed to be restored and refreshed. *Build the walls* again that your people might worship you in safety and in joy once more.

When these big things had been completed, then the detail of the worship could be renewed in its proper place. The Levitical system once again had meaning and purpose and so it could be carried on in the knowledge that God would be pleased to accept it.

What about you?

Perhaps, you are a Christian and you have sinned. Perhaps your sin is something that only you and a few others know about. Perhaps it is public and you cannot hold your head up in other people's company. How can you be restored? Well, you are not the first, or the worst to have sinned or fallen as a Christian. You may have fallen on the deck, but you cannot fall overboard. Your sin, no matter how great, will be forgiven and washed away by God, through the blood of his Son the Lord Jesus – that same Lord Jesus who loved you and died for you at the beginning of your Christian walk. What you must do is to come to God in exactly the same way that David did and take hold of his great promises by the same faith you did when you were first converted. Remember John's words: *If we confess our sin, he is faithful and just (because of what Jesus has done) to forgive us our sin and to cleanse us from all unrighteousness.* Who was John writing to? Christians! This is for you and for me. Whilst we can never take sin lightly as Christians, it can and is forgiven absolutely by the Lord upon our repentance.

What about the church looking on? How do we react when a brother or sister has fallen? Isn't it true that we can catch ourselves behaving like shameful hypocrites when we see a brother or a sister fall into sin? Isn't it all too true that we tut, and we gossip, and we jump to conclusions. We, whilst mouthing words like *there but for the grace of God go I,* judge and condemn our brother as if we could **never** do this. We are wrong. If the poet of Israel, the shepherd-king, the man after God's own heart can sin like this, then so can you and so can I. Never, never take that holier than you approach. Instead, once a sinning brother has repented, welcome him back. Assure him of your love. Give him as soon as possible a place and a role in the church. Watch over him, pray with and for him. Love him and shepherd him towards the flock of God and not away from it, considering yourselves that you also do not go astray. Our aim and our prayer should be to restore, as the Lord does, yet it seems that Christians are very good at the discipline side for that is cut and dried. It is much harder to forgive and restore, yet that is what we are commanded to do.

Lastly, going back to our allegory, Pilgrim was locked in Doubting Castle when we left him. What happened to him? Giant Despair intended hold him 'til he died. But after repenting and grieving over his sin, Christian found near to his heart a key called Promise. He used this to unlock the door of the castle and escape. Giant Despair was powerless to prevent him. Bunyan knew that once we lay hold of the promises of God's forgiveness, when we have repented of our sins, they cannot hold us anymore. Christian goes on his way a restored pilgrim: as free and as forgiven as he was at the Cross.

(Prologue)

These hands are stained with lust and blood

Bathsheba's soiled; Uriah's dead

God is displeased; his Name blasphemed

How could David be redeemed?

Lord to you alone I cry

Please forgive me 'ere I die.

Show mercy Lord on me I pray

Expiate my sin away

Wash me; cleanse me I implore

My filthy sin I now abhor

'Gainst you I've sinned - 'gainst you alone

Will you for my sins atone?

I ache with shame, for what I've done

In your sight Omniscient one

From mother's womb I've been impure

And I cannot concoct a cure

Purge with hyssop; cleanse like snow

May joy and gladness then follow

Hide your face from all my sin

Purify me deep within

Do not cast me, Lord away

Nor Spirit whom I've disobeyed

Restore to me salvation's joy

As your teacher now me employ

I would offer blood sacrifice

If I thought that would suffice

If in that you took delight

But you look for heart contrite

I humbly, abjectly repent

Forgive I pray - your wrath relent

Rebuild the walls of Zion now

May th' nations still before you bow.

Chapter 11

Beware the banana skin

Please read Psalm 42

It is a fact of life that often it is not the biggest hardships or tragedies or sins that do the most damage: it is the little things; it is the straw, not the iron bar that often breaks the camel's back. In this book I have deliberately focussed on the big events in Christian's life, but before we finish our book and Christian's journey, we need to look at some of the seemingly minor events, and the wearing accumulative effect they have. To look at them all individually would be too much, but to ignore them completely would be to do the story – and ourselves - a disservice.

In the course of his journey Christian meets with Atheist who laughs him to scorn for his hope. He meets the Flatterer who leads him astray, and traps him in his net. He also meets Ignorance who tries to undermine his faith and the necessity of his hard-walked pilgrimage. He meets By-Ends who seeks to assure him that the value of religion is only found in how you use it to gain what you want in this life.

In our Christian lives we have those times where we don't quite see the banana skin. We are going on nicely and then down we go. Old habits come back to haunt us, old sins and their consequences return. The impure fantasy re-appears. The enticing opportunity to do something we know we must not do is within reach. Or perhaps it is the taunts and the scoffing – the contemptuous dismissal of our faith. Perhaps we just get tired of swimming against the tide, or, to use the metaphor of our journey, of walking in the opposite direction to the majority of people; being in the narrow lane, alone, friendless and in the face of people hostile to us. We can usually deal with it, but now it has got to us and we have let ourselves down. Worse still, it is neither the first time, nor the thousand and first – and it won't be the last. And some little voice says inside: "Well it proves all along you are not saved; it proves you are a hypocrite. I hear again and again the little voice say to me: "It proves without doubt that you are the preacher who will be cast away". It is a truly awful and peace-shattering thought. It is a reminder of the devil's enmity and continual, debilitating warfare against us.

When we consider Psalm 42 the psalmist is just at that point. Perhaps he has slipped up, or tragedy has struck, or the way is just become too long and too hard, and he has reached a low, low point. Perhaps there is no direct trigger, but he's just had enough. We all can feel like this to one degree or another. For some Christians, mental depression also is real issue; a real illness, which can lead to a spiritual blackness where God feels far, far away. Whilst there are never any easy of off-pat answers, let us look at this psalm and take encouragement from it. Encouragement that someone else has been there before: encouragement that God made space to record their anguish in his book; encouragement there is some where to go in such a time of need.

Notice first though this one thing. The Book of psalms is actually divided into five books. This is the opening psalm of the second book. That would seem to be a deliberate choice of the editor of the five books of the psalms. Is it a reflection of the second book of the Pentateuch where the children of Israel are in trouble, groaning from their bondage? I think it may well be[58]. The point is God has recorded this psalm as surely as he has recorded the sufferings of his people. He still is recording

---

[58] The first psalm laid the foundation for the first book as Genesis lays the foundation for everything else in the bible, so here this psalm has that parallel to the Exodus. Psalm 73 is the first psalm of book 3, where it talks about the journey of the child of God, and the perils and lessons on the way. Such is the story of Leviticus. Psalm 90 is the beginning of Book 4 which talks about God's protection on the journey. Such is the story of Numbers. It is noteworthy that Book 4 contains a number of reflective psalms of that period. Book 5 starts with Psalm 107, which is a psalm of praise looking back at the story of the Children of Israel and a preparation for the future. Deuteronomy is Moses great sermon recalling exactly the same things. I wouldn't want to be dogmatic about it, but it might be a useful thing for further study.

the sufferings of every child of his. The positioning of this psalm I think shows it to be a psalm of great importance.

The psalmist's condition (vv1-4)

What do you see immediately the psalm opens? It is the heart of a man yearning for God. There is no spiritual soliloquy here; no deep and weighty doctrinal statements, or bold declaratives as many psalms have. There is just panting, groaning, sighing and lots of tears. There are no words, yet a message is being sent to God of deepest meaning. It is still a taboo idea but a very real one that a Christian is continually happy person. There is a poster which says "Wake up with a smile every morning – go to sleep with a coat hanger in your mouth". Whilst it is not true of any person alive that they are always happy, there is an expectation that living "on the vict'ry side" is all about a permanent smile and a happy disposition. That is not realistic, possible or scriptural. God's people suffer. In fact we could argue that Christians suffer more than any other group of people, because in addition to the ordinary woes suffered by all men under the curse of the fallen world, they suffer vindictively at the hands of those who hate God and his people. Never be down about being down. Neither look around and imagine everyone else is happier than you or has everything they (and you!) want. It is a fallacy – the devil hates all Christians equally and is busy ensuring their life is as hard as he can make it.

More than this we read that someone else is speaking but it only serves to make matters worse. "Where is your God", they say over and over and over again. As if what the writer is enduring is not hard enough (whether it is temptation; exile, imprisonment; or a sense of separation from God – perhaps due to sin or a feeling of guilt we do not know but they are all things that could cause it), there is this constant censure ringing in his ears. "Where is your God"? It is the taunt of our own self doubt, of the mocking world and the vindictive enemy of our soul, the devil.

Yet this phrase: "Where is your God", is one we do well to consider. It will unlock the key to the answers we seek. What are people saying and doing – or trying to do – when they see you down and rather than have a genuine compassion for you, make it worse with these words.

Firstly there are some who effectively are saying: I don't know where *your* God is, but here is *my* God. Your God is a silent God; aloof; vindictive, a punishing God. He wants you to be hurt. My God on the other hand is a God who lets me enjoy my life. He is a God I control. I can go to church, or not. I can keep the commandments or bend them if I need to. I am in charge; I live as I please, and as long as I basically do more good than bad, "the man upstairs" will doff his cap and give me the thumbs up.

Others use the phrase to effectively say: "Your God is not here". How many times do we hear so-called scientists talk in terms of millions of years of life on earth as evolutionary fact and say with equal certainty there can be no such thing as God? Journalists in our newspapers write mocking the idea of a Creator God. Others say your God is not here in the sense that they mean that God is not real but a comfort, a bit like a child's snugly, for those weak creatures who need a superstitious crutch. It's all a fairytale; it's all a nice story. Perhaps others will say it's an allegory – a fictional tale with a moral message to give us a moral framework. Then there are those who will say "Your God is not here" and mean it in the sense that there are lots of gods and lots of faiths and they all have a bit of something about them. The truth is a bit from everybody'd religion – your God is too narrow, too exclusive – you must broaden your views out: to insist of there being one God and one Saviour between God and man is bigotry and fantasy.

Then look at the taunt behind the claim. Have you ever asked: Why, if there is no God, or the God we believe is the wrong God, do people get so worked up about him? Why the taunts – why the blasphemy, if there is nothing to fear? Look at the venom the psalmist experiences in verse 3. Continually his taunters berate him. In verses 9 and 10 we read the enemies are oppressive and their taunts are as painful as the breaking of his bones, while they reproach him all day long. Now you have got to have a serious problem with God to be that venomous, but we find that this level of hatred of God is all too real don't we? In our country it exists, but in other places it is far, far worse. Why if he is not real do some hate God; the mention of his name and his people? The answer is obvious. God is real and they know it. God has put eternity in our hearts. All men know there is a God and a Heaven to gain and a Hell to shun because we are born with that knowledge. Our consciences witness against us all. It wasn't just the ancient Greeks in Athens who had a temple to every conceivable God, and then another to the "Unknown God" for the one they knew existed but didn't know who he was. We all do that. Reader, even if you are not a Christian, you know in your heart there is a God. You know that you want to go to Heaven when you die. You would have cold sweats at night if Hell opened its doors to receive you. But there is something in us which cavils at such a concept. We can know the truth but wilfully reject it. In fact that is the root and essence of the bible calls sin. Sin is not so much the breaking of the Ten Commandments – although it decidedly is that – it is the refusal to acknowledge God as God and to come to him humbly on his terms and ask him to forgive you for not coming earlier. It is the refusal to obey God's command that all should come to Jesus and ask forgiveness and for mercy. That refusal hardens our hearts and that rejection of God makes us rage against him because our conscience is at war with our will. Once we become Christians we become the victims of other people's inner torment; we have to bear this continual reproach. How do we cope with it? One answer is this: We cope with it by loving our tormentors as Christ does, and praying for them as Christ did. Some other answers follow in the psalm.

The Psalmist's conversations (vv4-10)

With all that turmoil going on in his mind, the psalmist is utterly cast down. He is at rock bottom. The accumulation of all these things have made him slip up and fall down. I want to emphasise this. This not an exercise in theory, this is a man who is pouring his soul to God in an agony of spirit. Think of Jesus in the Garden of Gethsemene; his agony of soul was too great for his body to bear and he sweat drops – great drops - of blood. The psalmist is pouring out his very core to God. Are you in that position reader? I would say there is probably not a Christian alive who has not come to this point in their journey, and for most, if not all, they have been here many times. Of course our circumstances and our temperament play a part in this but Bunyan writes a story of the typical pilgrim's journey. The Psalmist is not a great spiritual warrior; he is an ordinary man; one of the sons of Korah[59], whose name is not even mentioned.

---

[59] For an explanation of the Sons of Korah see Chapter 6

So, what do we do when we grind to this treacle-wading, snail pacing, stuttering, confused-at everything halt? Some just sit down and give up in frustration and bitterness. They focus on those who have let them down, hurt or crossed them. Some simply go and do something else – perhaps follow another path which seems easier, more enjoyable and less fraught, but end up spiritually nowhere: Bunyan writes of those. We see these people in the church and out of it, and it is a tragedy. What the Psalmist does is the simple thing, and yet the hard thing. He reasons spiritually and he prays. He has two conversations.

Firstly he talks with himself: Why are you cast down O my soul, and why are you disquieted within me? To use the literal interpretation the psalmist asks himself "why are you sinking on to your knees, as if you have no strength. Why is the ground around you sunken in? Why are your heart and your spirit roaring as men rushing upon their foes in a battle? The rebuke is in the questions isn't it? There is no need for all the rage and sadness and depression. Hope in God. He is in control. His countenance is upon me – it means he turns his face to look at me. He takes knowledge of what I am going through and there is that implied idea of empathy and comfort. I am remembered – I am not forgotten. Am I going to carry on making a racket and a commotion? No. God is here and that's enough.

But, secondly he talks to God, and he pours out his soul in naked honesty as a child to his parent. It is as if he is crying "Where have you been"? I needed you, and you had forgotten me – you (like me watching the football) were oblivious to me and my voice". The word "forgotten" means literally: "You mislaid me". What a charge to bring to God! Yet that is how he feels, and that is all too often how we feel isn't it when things go wrong; when we are low.

Here is my problem Lord, I am cast down. I have been cast down by the reproach – the verbal stripping away of my peace of mind, of my confidence as a human being and my name has been degraded and exposed. That is the meaning behind the word reproach that the psalmist uses. The constant snide remarks are wearing me down. The constant swimming against the tide is tiring me out. The continual battle against the enemy of my soul without and my own sinfulness within is too much. I need help: As my children used to say to me: "I need a carry." The psalmist (v 6) is wandering[60] – perhaps in a forced exile –around the land and he longs for the real and comforting presence of God.

The Psalmist's calmness (vv 8-11)

---

[60] W S Plumer, and others, thinks the reference to these places signifies the extent of the wandering the psalmist has had to do. There seems no obvious significance to the places apart from their distance apart, and perhaps their remoteness which only serves to increase the psalmist's sense of isolation. See pp496-7

Although the conversation with God ebbs and flows somewhat, towards the end of the psalm the trend of it is upwards. The Psalmist says to himself in effect: Although the billows are rolling over my head: though my enemies are stabbing away at me; though I feel like I am permanently in the funeral parlour; I will look up; I will stand up. Lord, I know you will constitute your lovingkindness again and lavish it upon me. You will order it to come to me so the literal words mean. You will fill my heart with hope and with a song. You will listen to my prayer and you will restore my life. William Jones comments: *In the* [remote] *land of the Hermons, He is as near to save thee as in ... the sanctuary.*[61] W. Graham Scroggie adds: *First the billows, then the blessings; first the sigh, then the song; first the mourning, and then the morning. No one who truly pants after God will fail to find him. Hope and you shall yet Praise.*[62] And at the end (v11) it is my countenance that has been turned. First God turned his face to me, but now I turn my face to look and it's as if our eyes meet, and the relationship is restored. I am out of the net; I am up on my feet. I am back on the path; I have gotten hold of my scroll, and, I am on my way again.

---

[61] The Preachers Homiletic Commentary Volume 11 p210
[62] The Preachers Homiletic Commentary Volume 2 p249

Finally

How do you and I make the psalmist's experience our own? It would be unhelpful to write down any kind of formula or recipe for success because we are all different and our circumstances are all different. The principles remain the same however. Firstly we must always remember that our doubts and fears are always the work of the enemy. We blame God for all our woes but he is not the author of them, he is the restrictor of them. He is not the instigator of our troubles, but the caretaker. It is the enemy of our souls who sends the Flatterer to deflect us; the Ignorant to undermine us and the Atheist to oppose us. The psalmist turns to God and cries in anguish – "you have mislaid me", but God hasn't done any such thing. Rather than blame God, we must stand and resist the devil.

Secondly we must realise that all trials have a twin purpose: God means to build us up and the devil means to trip us up. the success or failure of these trials rather depends on how we approach them; do they make us like the north wind close up, or like the sun open up to God? Often the very last thing we think of trials and in particular trials of mockery, and constant wearying reproach is that this is a spiritual trial at all. We see the physical circumstances not the hidden protagonist. We need to remember always we are on a pilgrimage and these circumstances are either going to turn us off the path or help us along it.

Then, we must realise that we own our behaviour – we are responsible for our actions – and our reactions. And it is truism that the closer we are to God the better our reactions will be, and the easier the trials will be to bear.

Lastly, we must always remember as of first importance that God is always for us and not against us. He does put our tears in his bottle. He does cradle us in his arms. He does love us with a tender, everlasting love and we can and we must always turn to him – even in the deepest anguish and not away from him in petulance. Petulance and unbelief and impatience will rob us of our peace. The question "why" is asked ten times in this psalm. It is how it is asked that makes it positive or negative; uplifting or downcasting. How can we not trust God for the daily little things, when we trust him with the eternal safety of our souls? The reason we don't as well as we should is because the devil who cannot rob us of our inheritance wants to rob us of our peace, and we let him when we take our eyes of the prize and focus on the little things. It was the little foxes that spoilt the vineyard (Song of Solomon 2:15). It was Peter's experience that when he looked at the wind and waves instead of Jesus that he began to sink (Matthew 14:30). Let those pictures be a warning and a comfort to us. Satan cannot destroy us. Satan cannot snatch us out of God's hands. So, put on that armour that God gave you for the fight (Eph 6); go and sit at the table God gave you for the feast (Psa 23:5) and march on a full stomach towards the Celestial City. Watch out for the banana skins and get there safely.

As pants the deer for desert brook

For you I crave and long and thirst

Why are you hidden from my look?

You know I need you most and first.

My vicious foes with no remorse

Mock and cavil at my tears

"Where is your God" - without a pause

They pile their hate upon my fears

I am kept far from your house

Where I once went with multitude

Yet now my feast is billows loud

Reproach and mourning are my food

You have forgotten me my God

I am cast down and drowning too

Why Lord have I been forgot?

When I've been busy loving you

Hold! Why am I so cast down

When God his kindness will command

I shall not fall – I shall not drown

His help: His love are in my hand

Chapter 12

Time to go Home

Please read Psalm 40[63]

Christian has one last part of his journey to go through. He comes on his journey in sight of the Celestial City, where his Lord and Saviour lives. But standing before him is a great River. He has to cross this River to get to the Celestial City. This is the last and the biggest test of all. The final battle of faith has to be fought out. After all is said and done will he be able to cross that river? Will the Lord he has been marching to see actually want to see him? Will he be allowed into the Celestial City at all? If not, what will happen to him? He knows he must cross the river, and he must cross it by walking through it. No one can take him across. As he begins to go down to the cold and wet chill of death itself he is all but overwhelmed by horror. His life flashes before him. He remembers in particular his failings and his sins. He begins to doubt that the Lord will really save him after all. He begins to convince himself that the very

---

[63] Reader, please note; Clearly there is the Messianic interpretation which is not included here, because I have deliberately restricted myself to looking at this psalm from David's viewpoint only, and in the context of this book.

fact that he is going through such difficulties is a sign that really he is not going to make it across at all.

David is facing a great dilemma of his own. We're not told what it is. Facing death is one strong possibility. Will God deliver him? What is the basis of his confidence? Is it his greatness, or his years of faithful service? No. It is his faith in God. That is what is going to give him his hope for the future. And so as he faces his big trial, he reviews his life and uses what God has done for him in the past as his hope base for what he needs God to do for him in the future. And so this psalm is a psalm of testimony. That testimony leads him to believe that the Lord will come to him and help him. This psalm is about David's spiritual hope. What gave him that hope? What sustained that hope? What does he hope for now?

What gave David his hope?

David starts the psalm by remembering his first great need. He pictures himself in a pit: horrible, slimy, sticky and smelly[64]. This is a spiritual picture – living a life of sin is like wallowing in the cesspit instead of swimming in the blue clean oceans. Furthermore he was trapped in it – he could not break out, climb out or walk out of this situation. When sin has a hold it does not let go. He was totally stuck.

---

[64] This actually happened to Jeremiah. See Jeremiah 38 vv1-13

He no doubt tried everything but failed to break free. What could he do now? One option is to ignore it all, and make the best of it, which is what many do. He could simply pretend sin wasn't important and carry on as if there was nothing wrong. Many do that also. But David was so aware of the filth of the sin he wallowed in, and was acutely aware of his need for cleansing, that he did the only thing he could do: he cried to the Lord. He cried to God - again and again. It appears that God did not seem to answer him straightaway. He *waited patiently for the Lord* to deliver and save him. This word *patiently* carries with it the sense of expectancy. It is as if David waits with his feet up, nice and relaxed, saying to himself "there is no rush; the Lord will come". David waited with trust and a certainty in his heart for the Lord to deliver him. In the Lord's good time he did. He lifted him out of that pit, pulled him out of the slime and mud and set him on a rock. We know (I Corinthians 10 v 4) *that rock was Christ.* In other words God forgave David his sins. He was a saved man. We have read enough of David's psalms by now to know he really understood that God alone could forgive and atone for his sins, and furthermore he was absolutely convinced that God had done so. There is no uncertainty in these verses. David's spiritual life started when he came to an end of himself, waited in the keenest of expectations for God to save, and deliver him. And so God did. He set him on the March to Zion – on the pilgrimage to the Celestial City. Notice that the Christian path is underpinned with a solid foundation that nothing can sweep away – *he put my feet upon a rock.* Notice also that the Christian path is a life of *steps.* In other words the Christian life is to be walked one step at a time – God's time. We thought about this in Psalm 23. We must not try to force the pace of our Christian lives, nor outstay the place where we are unwilling to move on. God has a time and a place for us, and we must follow him a step at a time, and embark on a life of trust. Jesus tells us not make great long-reaching plans, but to take life, a step at a time (Matthew 6 vv 25-34)[65]. Notice finally that the Christian's life is given by God; *He established my steps.* This word established is the same word used in Psalm 24 v 2, where David tells us that God established the earth upon the waters. All these things gave David his hope in the first place.

What sustained David's hope?

David's hope was sustained by his continuous relationship with God. God did not just save him, and then leave him. That is not God's way, any more than with creation itself. God does not only establish the world; he sustains it also. It is the same with David. God has saved him. Now God lives with him. David got on with living a life of praise to God, and for praise of God. David 's heart was always ready to

---

[65] See also James words in James 4 vv13-16

praise, even in the tough times. But notice it is God that puts the song into David's mouth. What kind of song? A song of praise to God, and this song is not just to be sung, it is to be lived. David makes the Lord his trust. Look at the way this phrase is written. This is a continuous trust for David. It is his habit, his way of life. It is the way he takes each established step on his pilgrimage. How does he do this? Firstly he goes on his way in a spirit of counting his blessings. Look at verse 5: *Many O Lord my God, are your wonderful works...* David interprets the events of his life in this sense; that God is ordering everything for his good. David as we know had many hardships, battles dangers and cares. He also made mistakes. But through it all he knew God was thinking of him, protecting and blessing him on his march.

What also sustained David is he never forgot how he was saved - verse 6 - and how he continually needed that forgiveness, which was a gift from God[66]. Furthermore the hallmark of David's relationship with God was that of obedience, which he knew was better than sacrifice[67]. The law he knew must be written on his heart, not just on the tablets of stone. Although the Old Testament is often thought of as full of Mosaic laws of do's and don't's, David

---

[66] See Psalm 51and the previous chapter
[67] I Samuel 15 vv 22

162

knew full well that what God wanted, and that was people who would love him freely and serve him from the heart. David knew a life like this would fulfil the law, just as Paul wrote later; *Love is the fulfilment of the law*[68], and he sought to live his life like this.

David has sustained his hope also by being faithful in testifying about God. He had not shunned proclaiming the truth (v9) at every opportunity. He had readily told others about God. He had clearly been ready to give his testimony. He had told of God's righteousness, faithfulness and salvation. How we should be ready, Peter writes, *to give a reason for the hope that is in us.* Do you do that? David was a faithful witness, in life and word to the greatness of his God. That is a really big challenge and example for us to follow in our lives here and now.

What was David hoping for now?

If we can join up the image of Christian crossing the river with David's own time when he drew near to die, these verses take on wonderful richness. We do not know, of course whether David was facing his actual death, but it is certain he was facing something of great difficulty. In times such as this what happens to us as Christians? Note these things from the last verses of this psalm:

---

[68] Romans 13 v 10

1. God seems to be far away (v 11).

David calls to God, but God doesn't appear to be there. David calls out in fear *do not hold back your tender mercies Lord.* Not now, for now I need to know you are with me. He needs to know God's kindness and truth. In times of temptation to despair we must remind ourselves of the truth. What truth is this? The truth of God's promises to us as his children. Those promises never fail, or fade or change. We must hold on to that at all times.

2. David remembers his forgiven sins as though they are not forgiven (v12, 13).

Look at how full of anguish these words are. Evils have surrounded me. My iniquities have overtaken me. They are so heavy that I can't lift my head up. I am overwhelmed. I am ashamed. I am in despair. When I look at my life I see more sins than there are hairs on my head. How can I be saved? Deliver me please O Lord! There are many times in our lives when we feel as if our repentance was a sham; when our turning to the Lord was just an emotional thing rather than a real event. Perhaps none more so than when we know we are about to cross the river; when eternity beckons. What a comfort to know that the man after God's own heart felt the same. Here is a man of course who committed great sins, but was told that they were forgiven. We are told the same, but it still doesn't stop the chilling, despairing thought that after all we have said and done, the Lord will say to us, when we knock at the gates of the Celestial City, "I never knew you". Is there a remedy? "He who comes to me," says Jesus, "I will never cast out. Even at the end of our lives we can still come to Jesus. Once we have come, no matter what mistakes we have made, we are eternally safe. Be assured Christian friend.

3. *David knows the devil and his minions are mocking his hope (v14, 15).*

David is aware that Satan wants him in hell. He does everything he can to make David loosen his grip on his hope. David prays against this. Whether our enemies are physical or not Satan is behind it, and he always has the same agenda: to make us give up our pilgrimage in despair. As we cross the river of death we are very vulnerable to thinking that God won't want us, won't save us, but God has not changed. The Son he sent to die for us won't let go of us now. David asks that Satan and his hosts would be put in despair themselves, driven back disappointed and confounded as they see again their own failure to pluck a child of God from his hands.

4. *David prays for fellow pilgrims in the same plight as he (v16).*

We seldom face this river alone. Perhaps there are others crossing it with us, or perhaps we are leaving loved ones behind. We should pray for them; that God would enable them also to rejoice in the hope that is theirs. Also we should pray that they might be enabled to magnify the Lord even though they are sad.

5. *David prays one final time for help and hope (v17).*

We can almost see David (as well as Christian) crossing the river. One last deep breath; one last tucking in the shirt and checking the hair is tidy, and away we go. "Poor and needy though I am yet the Lord thinks on me", he writes. This word: *think* means, *to plait or weave.* Even here God is calmly designing and making his own purposes to come to pass. The Christian is safe. David was safe. God will see to it. David is now in heaven for sure. Bunyan's character crossed the river safely and was received into the Celestial City. God will take us over the river of death and welcome us home to heaven with the words: *well done, good and faithful servant.* It is our task, privilege and joy to work to ensure we deserve to hear those words from our master, our friend, the one who loved us and gave himself for us.

One trial before I see my Lord
This deathly river now to ford
I'm overwhelmed with fear.
How will I know I'll safely cross,
And that my soul won't suffer loss?
Will I be welcome there?

I patiently waited once before
The Lord's name I learned to adore
He found me in the pit
He drew me up from miry clay
And set me going on my way
For heaven he made me fit.

I'm poor and needy as I cross
And so I look towards your Cross
Jesus remember me!
Do not delay to help me Lord
Keep the promise in your word
In mercy welcome me.

Bibliography

Blaiklock, E. M. (1977), Psalms for Living, Scripture Union, London

Bunyan, John (1678), The Pilgrim's Progress, Collins (1943 edition), London

Crossley, Gareth (2002), The Old Testament Explained and Applied, Evangelical Press, Darlington

Henry, Matthew (ed. Church, L. F. 1960), Commentary on the Whole Bible (Broad Oak edition), Marshall, Morgan & Scott, London

Kidman, Derek (1973 & 1975), Psalms 1-72 & Psalms 73-170, Inter Varsity Press, Leicester

Longman III, Tremper (1988), How to read the Psalms, Inter Varsity Press, Leicester

Plumer, William S (1867), Psalms (Geneva Series Commentary), The Banner of Truth Trust (reprint 1975), Edinburgh

170

Prime, Samuel (1859)   , The Power of Prayer – The New York Revival 1858, The Banner of Truth Trust (reprint 1991), Edinburgh

Scroggie, W. Graham (1949), Psalms (Volumes 1, 2 and 4) Know your Bible, Pickering & Inglis, London

Spurgeon, C. H. (unknown), The Treasury of David, Volumes 1, 2 and 3, MacDonald Publishing Company, Virginia, USA

Various authors (unknown), The Preachers Homiletic Commentary (31 Volumes), Baker Book House, Michigan, USA (Reprinted 1986)

White, John (1977), The Fight, Inter Varsity Press, Leicester

Made in the USA
Columbia, SC
21 December 2019

85439626R00102